Left **Ribeira da Janela islets** Middle **Capela dos Milagres, Machico** Right **The beach, Porto Santo**

Contents

Left **View from Bica de Cana** Right **Ponta de São Lourenço**

MADEIRA)

CHRISTOPHER CATLING

17

DORLING KINDERSLEY

LONDON • NEW YORK • MUNICH

Left **Funchal Casino** Middle **Flower sellers at Funchal market** Right **Casks of Verdelho Madeira**

A DORLING KINDERSLEY BOOK

www.dk.com

Produced by DP Services,
31 Ceylon Road, London W14 0PY

Reproduced by Colourscan, Singapore
Printed and bound in China by Leo Paper

First published in Great Britain in 2005
by Dorling Kindersley Limited
80 Strand, London WC2R 0RL
A Penguin Company

Reprinted with revisions 2007

A CIP catalogue record is available from
the British Library.

ISBN 1-40531-663-2
ISBN 978-1-40531-663-7

Within each Top 10 list in this book, no
hierarchy of quality or popularity is
implied. All 10 are, in the editor's
opinion, of roughly equal merit.

Contents

Madeira's Top 10

Cover: **Corbis** Neil Miller/Papilio cl; **Robert Harding Picture Library** H.P.Merton bl; **Photolibrary.com**
The Travel Library main. Back: **Corbis** Hubert Stadler tr; **DK Images** Linda Whitwam tc and tl.
Spine: **DK Images** Linda Whitwam.

MADEIRA'S TOP 10

MADEIRA'S TOP 10

TOP 10 Madeira Highlights

Madeira is an island of astonishing contrasts. From the big-city sophistication of the capital, Funchal, it is a short step to the primeval woodland that cloaks the dramatic cliffs and canyons of the island's interior. The fertility of Madeira's flower-filled gardens is in marked contrast to the aridity of the island's volcanic peaks. And nothing could be more different than the gentle rippling of the levadas (canals), which carry water into Madeira's deepest valleys, and the crash of the waves that dash the island's rocky shores. Madeira has been called a place where all the continents meet. It has something of them all – including snow.

1 Funchal Cathedral (Sé)

Hewn out of the island's volcanic rock and its abundant timber supplies, Madeira's cathedral is a monument to the faith and piety of the island's first settlers *(see pp8–9).*

2 Museu de Arte Sacra, Funchal

Trade contacts with Antwerp in the 15th century enabled Madeira's merchants to sell their sugar – so valuable that it was known as "white gold" – and buy the superb Flemish paintings and sculptures that fill this art museum *(see pp10–11).*

3 Adegas de São Francisco, Funchal

Madeira is renowned for its wines, famous for their complexity and depth of flavour. At this historic wine lodge you can sample different vintages and learn to be a Madeira connoisseur *(see pp12–13).*

4 Museu da Quinta das Cruzes, Funchal

Look inside a gracious Madeiran mansion, built on the site where the island's first ruler, João Gonçalves Zarco, had his home *(see pp14–17).*

Preceding pages **View of Curral das Freiras, with Pride of Madeira flowers in foreground**

Jardim Botânico, Funchal

The Botanical Gardens are a showcase for all the plants that thrive in the island's warm and humid climate, from jungle orchids to bristling cacti *(see pp20–23)*.

5 Mercado dos Lavradores, Funchal

The Farmers' Market is a bustling medley of colourful stalls positively bursting with exotic fruits, scented flowers and examples of local crafts *(see pp18–19)*.

7 Quinta do Palheiro Ferreiro

Two hundred years of cultivation have produced this magnificent all-seasons garden where the flowers of the world combine with the English flair for garden design *(see pp24–5)*.

8 Monte

Escape to a romantic world of gardens, tea-houses and cobbled walks, home to Emperor Charles I in exile. Afterwards, return to the capital on the exhilarating Monte toboggan run *(see pp26–7)*.

9 Curral das Freiras

During pirate attacks, the nuns of Santa Clara took refuge in this hidden green valley encircled by sheer cliffs – a place of breathtaking scenic beauty *(see pp30–31)*.

10 Pico do Arieiro

Feel on top of the world as you view the ridges and ravines of the island's mountainous interior from the summit of Madeira's third highest peak (1,818 m; 5,965 ft) *(see pp32–3)*.

🔟 Funchal Cathedral (Sé)

Save for a flurry of pinnacles at the eastern end, Funchal Cathedral's exterior is very plain. By contrast, the interior is lined with statues, paintings and gold-covered chapels; the ceiling is of spectacular knotwork inspired by Moorish geometry; and set in the floor are the tombs of early bishops and sugar merchants. Designed by Pêro Anes, assisted by master mason Gil Enes, the cathedral was begun in 1493. Consecrated in September 1514, when Funchal was officially granted city status, it was finally completed in October 1517.

Funchal Cathedral

🌐 The cathedral marks the social heart of Funchal. The pavement cafés to the south (the Café Funchal and the Café Apolo) are popular meeting places for people who live and work in the city centre, and great places to relax and simply watch the world go by.

✪ The cathedral is a functioning religious building, and visits are not encouraged during services (weekdays at 8am, 8.30am, 11.15am and 6pm; Sundays at 8am, 9am, 11am, 5pm and 6pm). If you go to a service, you will be able to see the normally dark interior of the church lit up.

- *Largo da Sé*
- *Map P3*
- *Open 9am–12.15pm, 4–6pm daily*
- *Free*

Top 10 Features

1. West Portal
2. Narthex and Baptistry
3. Nave and South Aisle
4. North Aisle
5. Ceiling
6. South Transept
7. Sanctuary
8. Seating in the Sanctuary
9. Altarpiece
10. East End

1 West Portal

King Manuel I of Portugal (1495–1521) helped to fund the construction of the cathedral, and it is his coat of arms *(above)* over the Gothic doorway. The rose window above the crown is carved from rust-red local basalt.

2 Narthex and Baptistry

The vestibule to the church is paved with worn, 16th-century tomb slabs of black basalt. A wall plaque *(right)* records the visit of Pope John Paul II on 12 May 1991. To the left is the massive 16th-century font of the Gothic baptistry.

3 Nave and South Aisle

Here, floor memorials to bishops and merchants carved in marble and basalt reflect the 16th-century Portuguese style.

The Portuguese word for cathedral is Sé, which means "seat", a reference to the bishop's throne, the symbol of his authority.

5 St James by Dieric Bouts

This study of St James was probably painted in Bruges in the 1470s. The saint's gorgeous scarlet cloak and the flower-filled meadow in which he stands are typical of Flemish master Dieric Bouts' love of colour and naturalistic detail.

6 Deposition by Gerard David

The Virgin's face shows sadness and resignation as her Son is taken down from the Cross in the central panel of this triptych of 1518 (below). The side panels depict the donors – Simon Acciaiuoli, a merchant from Florence (with St Bernardino of Siena), and his wife Maria (with St James).

7 Annunciation by Joost van Cleve

The fruits of Europe's expanding commercial connections can be seen in this serene painting of around 1515: Mary's feet rest on an oriental carpet, and the lilies symbolizing her purity are standing in a Delft jar.

8 St Philip and St James by Pieter Coecke van Aelst

Here (above), the donors, pictured kneeling on either side of the central panel, have been identified as Simão Gonçalves de Câmara, grandson of Zarco, and his wife Isabel.

9 St Anne and St Joachim

This fascinating early 16th-century painting of the Antwerp School (right) is reputed to show King Ladislaw III of Poland (see p37) and his wife Senhorina Eanes. Known as Henry the German, the king gave up his crown and became a farmer on Madeira in 1454.

10 The Machico Adoration

Rich in detail, this anonymous painting of around 1518 from the church at Machico (see p87) depicts Madeiran merchants and landowners in the guise of the Three Kings, with their servants.

Flemish Art

Madeiran art patrons would probably not have visited Antwerp or Bruges to sit for their portraits. Instead, they might have sent a sketch (perhaps drawn by one of the island's architects or masons) or perhaps relied on a friend to give the artist an accurate verbal description. In any case, exact likeness was not the artist's aim. Following the Mannerist tendency, the painter of the Machico Adoration emphasizes distinctive facial features – a large nose or a double chin – in order to give greater character to his subjects.

🏛10 Adegas de São Francisco, Funchal

Plenty of places on Madeira offer wine tastings, but none will give you such a solid introduction to the history of its unique wine. With its heavy ancient beams and its cobblestone courtyards, the Adegas de São Francisco feels as old as time. It is set in the surviving parts of a 16th-century Franciscan friary, most of which was demolished when Portugal passed its laws banning religious orders in 1834. The premises were acquired by the Blandy family (see p25) in 1840 and have been used ever since for making Madeira wine.

Sampling Madeira wine at the Max Romer Tasting Bar

🔵 To the west of the wine lodge, there is an outdoor café in the cloister of the São Francisco friary, now a delightful public garden.

🟢 You can wander in and out of the wine lodge whenever it is open. Wines may be sampled for free in the Max Romer Tasting Bar without booking a tour.

- Avenida Arriaga 28
- Map P3
- 291 740 110
- Open 9:30am–1pm, 2:30–6:30pm Mon–Fri, 10am–1pm Sat (Max Romer Tasting Bar also open for lunch)
- Admission free
- Tours: 10:30am, 2:30pm, 3:30pm, 4:30pm Mon–Fri, 11am Sat. €4
- In-depth vintage tours: 4:30pm Wed, Fri. €6

Top 10 Features

1. Courtyard
2. 17th-century Wine Press
3. Goatskins
4. Attics
5. Wine Shop
6. Wine Museum
7. Max Romer Tasting Bar
8. Vintage Room
9. Shopping Arcade
10. The "Oldest Street"

1 Courtyard

The romantic inner courtyard of the wine lodge is shaded by some of the island's tallest banana trees *(above)*. It is ringed by three storeys of attics with wisteria-draped external balconies supported on massive timber brackets.

2 17th-century Wine Press

On the guided tour you will be shown a traditional wine press carved with the Jesuit symbol of a cross within a triangle. The Jesuits ran the island's wine trade until the late 18th century. English and Scottish merchants then took it over.

3 Goatskins

Wine made all over the island was brought for sale to Funchal. Porters called *borracheiros* sipped from the 40-litre loads of wine that they carried in goatskins.

4 Attics

Massive timbers support three storeys of ventilated attics *(below)*. Wines here are aged in casks warmed only by the sun, a method known as "Canteiro" that produces quality wines.

For more on Madeira wines See pp58–9

5 Wine Shop
The rustic-styled shop has shelves fashioned from old wine casks. On sale here is a large selection of wines by all the producers in the Madeira Wine Company under the labels Blandy's, Cossart Gordan, Leacock's and Miles. Spirits and Madeira cakes are also sold.

6 Wine Museum
Framed letters of appreciation from kings and queens, emperors, presidents and prime ministers – all of them lovers of good Madeira wine – line the walls of the museum at the heart of the lodge. Also on display here are leather-bound ledgers recording every sale going as far back as the 18th century.

7 Max Romer Tasting Bar
The delightfully sunny murals of grape-growing and harvesting that cover the walls of the tasting bar on the ground floor were painted in 1922 by the German artist Max Romer (1878–1960).

8 Vintage Room
Within the Vintage Room, precious wines are stored by date and kept locked behind bars. Madeira wines dating back to 1908 (and costing €698 a bottle) can be sampled here. Those who cannot afford the above can try moderately priced, but nevertheless appealing, 1970s vintages.

9 Shopping Arcade
In a sign of the times, the old cooper's yard was recently converted into a shopping arcade. However, the Madeira Wine Company still employs coopers to patch and mend 100-year-old barrels. The coopers use traditional methods, mixing new and old oak.

10 The "Oldest Street"
The street that runs up the eastern side of the wine lodge dates from the 1400s, in the early days of Madeira's settlement. Wine barrels were once dragged across the cobbles on a sledge going to and from the harbour.

Madeira Wine
Madeira wine has two defining characteristics. First, like sherry and port, it is "fortified" by the addition of brandy at the end of the fermentation process. Second, it is heated during production. The benefits of heating were discovered when wines left on board ship after a round trip to the equator were found to have developed a new depth and complexity of flavour. In time, winemakers worked out how to recreate the effect by maturing the wine in lofts heated by the sun, without the need for a sea journey. (See also p59 on estufagem.)

Madeira's wine industry was nearly wiped out when the vines were attacked by mildew in 1851, and by phylloxera (vine louse) in 1872.

13

🔟 Museu da Quinta das Cruzes, Funchal

Madeira's early settlers built their homes on the heights above the harbour so that they could see pirate ships approaching. The Quinta das Cruzes is just such a mansion. Originally built by Captain Zarco (see p36), it was rebuilt in the 19th century as the elegant home of the Lomelino family, and is now a museum full of antiques and fine art. An excursion to the Quinta can be combined with a visit to the Convento de Santa Clara (see pp16–17), a short walk away.

Museu da Quinta das Cruzes

🍵 There's a delightful teahouse in the courtyard of the Universo de Memórias (itself worth a visit), opposite the entrance to the Quinta. Sip tea by a fountain, on a terrace ringed by flowers and climbing plants.

🎵 Concerts are often held in the Museu da Quinta das Cruzes; look out for posters in the ticket office.

It's a steep climb to the museum, and there's no bus – so you might want to take a taxi.

- Calçada do Pico 1
- Map N2
- 291 740 670
- 10am–12:30pm, 2–5:30pm Tue–Sat, 10am–1pm Sun
- Admission €2

Top 10 Features

1. Archaeological Park
2. Manueline Windows
3. Orchid Garden
4. Chapel
5. Trade Goods
6. Drawing Rooms
7. *Picnic* by Tomás da Anunciação
8. Palanquin
9. Sugar Box Furniture
10. Silver Collection

1 Archaeological Park

The gardens to the south of the Quinta *(above)* serve as an outdoor museum of ancient masonry. One prominent relic is the base of Funchal's pillory, erected in 1486. Until 1835, criminals were chained to the pillory and whipped.

2 Manueline Windows

The stone window frames set up in the garden *(right)* are fine examples of a style inspired by the voyages of discovery made during the reign of King Manuel I of Portugal (1495–1521). They are carved with knotted ships' ropes, lions and a porter carrying a goatskin full of wine on his head.

3 Orchid Garden

A stately old dragon tree *(see p21)* thrusts its fleshy limbs through the roof of the shade house at the rear of the Quinta garden, where tier upon tier of tropical orchids are grown for use as cut flowers.

4 Chapel
The chapel contains the tomb of Urbano Lomelino *(above)*, an early sugar merchant. His descendants moved it here when they acquired the estate in 1678.

5 Trade Goods
Before you enter the main house, there's an exhibition of trade goods from the 19th-century Portuguese empire, including a silk bedspread embroidered with tropical flowers, an ivory carving of a Buddha-like baby Jesus, and an altar frontal featuring tigers.

entrance

Key

| | Ground Floor |
| | First Floor |

7 *Picnic* by Tomás da Anunciação
Picnic (above), by the founder of the Portuguese school of landscape art, dates from 1865. The family of the 2nd Count of Carvalhal is depicted on their Quinta do Palheiro Ferreiro estate *(see p24)*.

8 Palanquin
A palanquin, used in the 19th century to carry a wealthy lady around Funchal, is displayed in the basement. Also here are a series of English satirical engravings poking fun at Funchal's well-fed priests and over-dressed officials.

6 Drawing Rooms
Zarco's original mansion was a busy working farm and administrative centre. The Lomelino family radically remodelled the house in the early 19th century, filling the well-proportioned drawing rooms with English Chippendale furniture and fine paintings.

Captain Zarco: Lord of the Isles

João Gonçalves (nicknamed Zarco – "Squinter" – after he lost an eye at the Battle of Ceuta in 1415) planted the Portuguese flag on Porto Santo in 1419, and on Madeira in 1420. In 1425 he returned with people, seeds and tools to live on Madeira. Zarco ruled the island's south-western half, while his fellow captain, Tristão Vaz, ruled the northeast from Machico. Zarco's half proved to have the better harbour, which became the island's capital. He died in 1467, at the ripe age of 80.

9 Sugar Box Furniture
Brazilian sugar put an end to the Madeiran sugar trade. The mahogany boxes used to transport the sugar were turned into the robust chests *(right)* seen in the basement.

10 Silver Collection
A rich collection of historic silver is on show in the basement. Highlights include a pair of silver-and-ebony Mexican slave figures (late 18th-century) and two silver-and-coral British baby's rattles (mid 18th-century).

Left **Lower choir** Middle **17th-century carpet tiles, Santa Clara Church** Right **Upper choir**

Convento de Santa Clara, Funchal

1 Gateway
The arms of the Order of St Francis are carved on the 17th-century stone roundel above the ancient wooden doors of the convent gateway. Ring the bell here to be admitted. ✆
Calçada de Santa Clara 15
• Map N2 • 291 742 602
• Open 10am–noon, 3–5pm Mon–Sat, 10am–noon Sun • Admission €2

Santa Clara Convent

convent's first abbess, Isabel de Noronha, and her sister, Constança. As a sign of their humility, these high-born ladies (whose grandfather was Zarco – *see p36*) chose to be buried in a corridor where nuns would walk across their graves each day.

2 Cloister
This peaceful spot provided access to chapels and oratories where the nuns could pass the day in prayer. From here you can admire the cupola of the convent's bell tower, decorated with rare 17th-century blue, white and gold ceramic tiles.

3 Abbess's Grave
A gravestone with Gothic script marks the burial place of the

Cloister

4 Upper Choir
Green Moorish tiles cover the floor of this long room, with its knotwork ceiling and gilded altar housing a statue of the Virgin. This choir was the place of daily prayer for the first community of Poor Clare nuns (the sister order to the Franciscans), who came to Santa Clara from Portugal in 1497.

5 Lower Choir
The lower choir is lined with wooden choir-stall chairs dating from 1736, carved with winged cherubs and amusing animal heads. The painted throne was reserved for the use of the bishop and the head of the Franciscan order when either visited the convent.

6 Grille
Through the iron grille set in the eastern wall of the lower choir the congregation could hear the sweet singing of the nuns, and the nuns could hear the priest say mass. The nuns had no other contact with the outside world.

From the Quinta das Cruzes (see pp14–15), take the Calçada do Pico towards Funchal; the convent will be on your right.

7 Zarco Monument

A coffin-shaped box at the eastern end of the lower choir is a replica of the monument that once stood in the main church over Zarco's grave *(see p15)*. It was moved in 1762 because priests kept tripping over it.

8 Calvary

The large painting of the crucified Christ at the west end of the lower choir served to remind the nuns that their hardships were as nothing compared with his sufferings. Even more poignant is the realistic 17th-century wooden statue of Christ laid in the altar below, as if in his tomb.

9 Church

The public part of the church is covered in decorative 17th-century carpet tiles of great intricacy. The magnificent silver tabernacle on the altar dates from 1671.

10 Monuments

At the back of the church, the stone sarcophagus resting on crouching lions marks the grave of Zarco's son-in-law, Martim Mendes de Vasconcelos (d.1493). Zarco himself (who died in 1467 – *see pp14, 36*) lies buried in front of the high altar, but his tomb slab is hidden beneath a modern wood floor.

Top 10 Dates in Santa Clara's History

1. 1476: convent founded
2. 1493: church completed
3. 1497: nuns move in
4. 1566: nuns flee pirates
5. 1671: tabernacle unveiled
6. 1736: choir stalls carved
7. 1797: artists paint church
8. 1834: Portugal bans religious orders
9. 1890: last nun dies
10. 1927: school founded

Santa Clara Church

Santa Clara Convent is surrounded by high walls, built to shield the nuns from prying eyes, and to keep them focused on their religious duties without the distractions of the outside world. In the past, the only part of the convent open to the public was the church, with its magnificent silver tabernacle, dating from 1671, and its marble-and-gold altar. Because of its beauty and serenity, Santa Clara Church is a very popular choice for weddings.

Bell Tower
The minaret-like bell tower reflects the cultural influence of Moorish Seville, where the tiles decorating the onion-shaped dome were made.

High altar with silver tabernacle, Santa Clara Church

🔟 Mercado dos Lavradores, Funchal

The bustling and colourful Mercado dos Lavradores is more than just a market; it is one of the social hubs of Madeira, a meeting place for people from all over the island, who come from the country by bus to shop and to sell their wares. The prices charged here are cheaper than those found in most of the supermarkets that are springing up all over Madeira – and who could resist buying fresh fruit, flowers or herbs from stallholders who make such efforts in creating their colourful displays?

Wickerwork, ground floor, Mercado dos Lavradores

🍴 For a tasty morsel, head for the hole-in-the-wall bars found around the outside of the market hall.

👁 Visit the fish market in the morning.

- Rua Profetas
- Map P4
- Open 7am–5pm Mon–Thu, 7am–8pm Fri, 7am–3pm Sat
- Free

Top 10 Features
1. The Market Hall
2. Leda and the Swan
3. Tile Pictures
4. Flower Sellers
5. Ground Floor
6. Cobbler
7. Fruit and Veg
8. Herbalist
9. Fish Market
10. Butchers and Bars

1 The Market Hall
This Art Deco hall was designed in 1937 by Edmundo Tavares (1892–1983). Though built from modern materials, its colours echo the grey and rust-red basalt of traditional Madeiran architecture.

2 Leda and the Swan
To the right of the entrance porch, a tile picture shows the market as it was at the turn of the 20th century *(above)*, with stalls under canvas awnings and stallholders in traditional costume. The fountain in the picture, topped by a marble statue of *Leda and the Swan*, has survived and is now in the town hall courtyard (see p42).

3 Tile Pictures
More tile pictures adorn the entrance porch. The work of artist João Rodrigues and made in 1940, they depict stallholders and the coat of arms of Funchal (featuring five sugar cones in a cross).

4 Flower Sellers
Today's flower sellers still wear traditional clothes. These are as colourful and eye-catching as their tropical orchids, bird-of-paradise plants, lilies and flamingo flowers *(below)*.

5 Ground Floor

In the arcades surrounding the central courtyard you can shop for leather bags and wickerwork, *fado* tapes, Madeira wine and honey cake. Farmers up from the country for the day sell bread, bunches of herbs and seasonal fruits from upturned crates.

6 Cobbler

As well as bargain leather bags, you can also buy handmade – and hard-wearing – Madeiran-style ankle boots and stylish natural leather sandals from Barros e Abreu *(left)*. The stall of this cobbler is located on the right-hand side of the entrance.

7 Fruit and Veg

Upstairs is the domain of the fruit and vegetable sellers, packed with colourful and sweet-smelling local produce. As you negotiate the narrow aisles, don't be surprised to be offered a free slice of mango, passion fruit or blood-red tomarillo as you pass, in the hope that you will linger and buy.

8 Herbalist

On the first floor near the stairs, one stall is devoted to fresh and dried herbs, all carefully labelled. There are bunches of feverfew for headaches, and fennel and eucalyptus sweets to soothe a cold.

9 Fish Market

If the fruit stalls are a taste of the Garden of Eden, the noisy fish market *(right)*, in the basement, looks like a scene from hell, with its knife-wielding stallholders in blood-stained aprons, hacking into tuna and *espada* fish.

10 Butchers and Bars

The butchers' shops, selling fresh, cooked and dried meat and sausages, are in a separate area reached from streets around the market hall. Ringing the perimeter of the hall are hole-in-the-wall bars, where shoppers and market workers snack on little dishes of garlic-flavoured beans, salty olives or sweet custard pastries.

The Fruits of Madeira

In Funchal's market, even the commonplace can take you by surprise: the tiny honey-scented bananas, no bigger than your finger, are the best you will ever taste. Ignore shiny imported apples and tomatoes in favour of flavoursome varieties that have been grown on the island for centuries. Now is your chance to taste lantern-shaped *pitanga* (Brazilian cherries), sugar cane, prickly pears, loquats, custard apples, guava, pawpaw, passion fruit, pomegranate and quince – all grown locally.

⑩ Jardim Botânico, Funchal

As well as being a place where avid plant lovers can learn all about the astonishing range of plants that thrive in Madeira's warm and humid climate this is also a great spot just to relax and enjoy the visual richness of the immaculately maintained flower beds. The gardens occupy the grounds of an estate that once belonged to the Reid family (founders of the world-renowned Reid's Palace Hotel) and, with a practised eye for a good building site, they chose to build their mansion on a sunny slope blessed with panoramic views

The outdoor café in the Jardim Botânico

🍴 There is a café in the grounds set around a series of pretty lotus- and lily-filled ponds.

🐸 Children will enjoy looking out for the frogs that live below the pondweed.

Some of the best views are to be had from the "Lovers' Cave" at the topmost point of the garden.

Entry to the Jardim Botânico also includes admission to the Jardim dos Loiros, or Parrot Park (see p53). Orchid fans shouldn't miss the Jardim Orquídea (see p56), a short, if steep, walk away.

• Quinta do Bom Sucesso, Caminho do Meio
• Map H5
• 291 211 200
• Open 9am–5:30pm daily
• Admission €3

Top 10 Features

1. Natural History Museum
2. Native Plants
3. Valley View
4. Cacti and Succulents
5. Carpet Bedding
6. Economic Plants
7. Medicinal Plants
8. Topiary Garden
9. Seaside Plants
10. Parrot Park

1 Natural History Museum

The Quinta do Bom Sucesso ("Mansion of Good Fortune") *(below)*, built in the late 19th century by the Reid family *(see pp37, 112)*, was bought by the Madeiran government in 1952. It was opened in 1960 as the Natural History Museum.

2 Native Plants

So many plants have been introduced to the island that it is useful to be reminded of native species. Those growing in beds alongside the museum *(above)* include bold and colourful Madeiran geraniums and giant golden buttercups.

3 Valley View

The western edge of the garden (furthest from the entrance) has views over the green, canyon-like João Gomes Valley *(below)* Though crossed by a road bridge, this is an important wildlife corridor. Huge, ancient and gnarled parasol pines, with twisted branches and scaly bark, cling to the rocks alongside the *miradouro* (viewing point) that overlooks the valley.

The Botanical Gardens are 3 km (2 miles) northeast of Funchal, on the route of town buses 30 and 31.

Cacti and Succulents
This part of the garden is popular with children for its Wild West look *(above)* and for the many spiders that use the thorns of the cacti as supports for their intricate webs.

Jardim Botânico

Carpet Bedding
The purple, red, green, yellow, white and gold diamonds, lozenges and circles of this much-photographed part of the garden *(left)* demonstrate the richness and variety of colour to be found just in the leaves of plants.

Economic Plants
If you cannot tell a mango tree from an avocado, this is the place to learn. The plants grown here are used for food, fibre, oil or dye. Among them are several whose names we know but may never have seen – such as coffee, cocoa, sugar cane, cotton and papaya.

Medicinal Plants
Staff carry out research using the plants grown in this section to find herbal remedies for maladies from headaches to rheumatism.

Seaside Plants
Though not the most colourful or spectacular varieties, Madeira's many coastal plants must be admired for their tenacity. Most of them manage to grow on rocky cliffs or sandy shores, with minimal fresh water and a regular soaking in brine.

Topiary Garden
This knot garden *(above)* is made of clipped box, and planted with shrubs that can be cut into spirals, pyramids, chess pieces and animal shapes.

Parrot Park
The closer you get to the southern part of the garden, the less you will be able to avoid the squawks of the rare and exotic birds that are housed in the Parrot Park *(left)*.

Dragon Trees
If ever a plant looked like its name, the dragon tree *(Dracaena draco)* is it. The fleshlike branches have scaly grey bark that looks and feels reptilian, while the leaves are like claws or talons. When cut, the tree "bleeds" a vivid red sap which sets to form a resinous gum known as Dragon's Blood, once highly prized as a dye (it turns cloth purple). Long before Portugal colonized Madeira, sailors came here to harvest the sap of these strange trees, which still grow wild in Madeira, the Canary Islands and Cape Verde.

Some of the best views are to be had from the "Lovers' Cave" at the topmost point of the garden.

Left **Madeiran geranium** Middle **Pride of Madeira** Right **Giant buttercups**

Plants on Madeira

1 Madeiran Geranium
The Madeiran geranium, also known as cranesbill *(Geranium maderense)*, has become a popular garden plant all over Europe because of its shrubby stature, feathery leaves and large purple-veined magenta flowers.

2 Pride of Madeira
Pride of Madeira *(Echium candicans)* is almost the island's symbol. Blooming with an abundance of long-lasting powder-blue flower spikes at exactly the time of year (from December to March) when other flowers are shy, it adorns the island's roadsides, notably around the airport.

3 Lily-of-the-valley Tree
You could pass this shrub *(Clethra arborea,* or *folhado* in Portuguese) nine months out of twelve and not even notice it, but from August to October it is a stunner, hung all over with sweet-smelling clusters of bell-like flowers of purest white.

Madeiran juniper

4 Tree Heath
Related to heather, and with similar pink bell-like flowers, Madeira's tree heaths *(Erica arborea)* can grow to a quite prodigious size; a carbonized tree heath trunk in Madeira's Natural History Museum *(see p20)* probably lived for several hundred years. Tree heath branches are used locally for fencing and windbreaks.

5 Giant Buttercups
Madeira's subtropical climate seems to encourage plants to turn into giants. Here, Poinsettias grow 4 m (12 ft) tall, and heaths are trees rather than shrubs. This tall shrubby buttercup *(Ranunculus cortusifolia)* is a very handsome plant that looks good anywhere.

6 Scented Bay
The essential flavouring ingredient in Madeira's national dish, *espetada* (beef kebabs), is the scented bay *(Laurus azorica,* or *loureiro* in Portuguese). It has aromatic evergreen leaves and grows abundantly in the wild.

7 Madeiran Juniper
Confusingly called *cedro* (cedar) in Portuguese, the dark wood of the Madeiran juniper has a rich patina that can be readily seen in the knotwork ceilings of Funchal Cathedral *(see p9)*, Santa Clara Convent *(see p16)* and the church in Calheta *(see p82)*.

Ironwood
8 *Apollonius barbujana* (in Portuguese, *barbusano*) is one of the main constituents of Madeira's native evergreen forest. Its billowing clouds of fresh lime-green leaves contrast with the deep green of previous years' growth.

Stink Laurel
9 The Portuguese took a heavy toll of the huge and ancient laurel trees (*Ocotea foetens*, or *til* in Portuguese) after they arrived on the island in 1420. Felled trunks were shipped to Portugal and Spain for shipbuilding; the ships of the Spanish Armada were largely built from this wood.

Madeiran Mahogany
10 Madeira's museums are full of fine furniture made from *vinhático (Persea indica)*, the mahogany-like wood that grows to a great height and girth in the woods. So valuable and costly was sugar in the 15th century that it was shipped to Europe in chests made of this wood.

Top 10 Wild Plants to Spot on a Walk

1. Viper's bugloss
2. Saucer plant (House leek)
3. Navelwort
4. Downy thistle
5. Shrubby sow thistle
6. Ice plant
7. Bilberry
8. Foxglove
9. Dog violet
10. Fleabane

Madeira: World Heritage Site

The primeval woodland that cloaks much of Madeira's mountainous interior is the remnant of the scented laurel forest that covered much of southern Europe until the last Ice Age (which ended around 10,000 years ago). Only on Madeira, the Canaries, the Azores and in tropical west Africa was the climate warm enough for these subtropical trees and shrubs to survive. Known in Portuguese as laurisilva *(laurel wood), they are a precious link with the past. UNESCO designated a large area of the island's natural forest as a protected World Heritage Site in December 1999.*

Primeval woodland

For more Madeiran flowers **See p65**

23

Quinta do Palheiro Ferreiro

The unmistakably English character of the Quinta do Palheiro Ferreiro was stamped on the estate by its first owner, the wealthy Count of Carvalhal, whose love of English landscapes led him to include woodland and grassy meadows when the estate was laid out in 1804. Bought by John Blandy, an English wine merchant, in 1885, the Quinta has remained in the same family ever since, greatly enriched by the plants that Mildred Blandy imported from China, Japan and her native South Africa.

Pink flowers and leaves of the cymbidium orchid

🍵 The newly built Tea House, serving delicious home-made cakes, stands at the lower end of the garden, bordering an area of the estate which is now run as a golf course *(see p48)*.

🛈 Visitors should note that the house is closed to the public.

- Caminho da Quinta do Palheiro 32, São Gonçalo
- Map H5
- 291 793 044
- 9am–4pm Mon–Fri
- Admission €8 (children €4)

Top 10 Features
1. The Long Avenue
2. Stream Garden
3. The Sunken Garden
4. The Chapel
5. Long Borders
6. The Terrace
7. The Old House
8. Lady's Garden
9. Hell Valley
10. Camellia Walk

The Long Avenue
Plane trees and giant camellias, many planted 200 years ago, line the avenue. The crimson, pink and white flowers are at their best from November to April, before the white arum lilies and pretty blue agapanthus take over.

Stream Garden
The stream you cross to enter the garden is fed by a spring. Lined by azaleas, rhododendrons and scarlet tritonias, and crossed by ornamental bridges, it attracts bathing robins and blackbirds.

The Sunken Garden
Water lilies fill the little pool at the centre of this pretty garden *(above)*. Tall cypresses mark its corners; topiary shapes flank its four sets of stone steps. In the borders, gazanias mix with beetroot-red house leeks.

The Chapel
The striking Baroque chapel has Venetian-style windows and a plasterwork ceiling depicting Christ being baptized in the River Jordan by John the Baptist.

The Quinta is 8 km (5 miles) from the centre of Funchal, on the route of town bus 37.

Long Borders
5 Typically English herbaceous border plants, such as delphiniums and day lilies, are mixed with tender and exotic orchids, and angel's trumpets (daturas). Climbing roses and jasmine are draped over arches so that you catch the heady scent as you pass.

Quinta do Palheiro Ferreiro

The Terrace
6 Paved with tiny sea-worn pebbles, the terrace offers a good view of the house (no admission) that John Blandy built in 1885, successfully blending English and Madeiran architectural styles.

The Old House
7 Now a luxurious hotel (see p113), the Casa Velha was originally a hunting lodge. Archduchess Leopoldina of Austria stayed here on her way to marry Pedro I of Brazil in 1817.

Hell Valley
9 Despite its name, this valley is a delightful tangle of bamboo, tree ferns, native woodland and creepers, with an understorey of beautiful acanthus plants.

Lady's Garden
8 The *Jardim da Senhora (above)* has topiary nesting birds and vintage trees, including a rare old Madeiran *til* tree (see p23), two canary pines and a weeping *Saphora japonica*, whose corkscrew limbs and delicate leaves cascade to the ground to form a natural green veil.

Camellia Walk
10 Look out for the stone circle called Avista Navios ("Place for Viewing Ships"), where there is a clear view all the way down to the harbour.

The Blandy Family
The first John Blandy (1783–1855) arrived in 1807 as quartermaster in General Beresford's army, which had been posted to Madeira to defend the island against attack from Napoleon. Blandy returned in 1811, and made his fortune supplying the ships that called at Funchal's busy port. His eldest son, Charles Ridpath, bought up all existing stocks of wine on the island when mildew caused grape harvests to fail in 1852. This bold move enabled the family to dominate the wine trade from then on.

The name Palheiro Ferreiro literally means "blacksmith's hut". Perhaps long ago a blacksmith chose this spot for his forge.

TOP 10 Monte

*Like the hill stations of colonial India, Monte (literally, "Mount") developed ͏
the late 18th century as a genteel and healthy retreat from the heat, smells ͏
noise and commercial activity of the capital. Funchal's suburbs now spread ͏
their tentacles all the way up to Monte, but there is still a sense of escaping fro ͏
the city and entering a world set apart. The cool, clear air is filled with birdson ͏
Few cars intrude onto the cobbled streets, and lush gardens are everywhere ͏
lushest of all, the extraordinary Monte Palace Tropical Garden (see pp28–9)*

The Monte cable car

🕐 You can get to Monte
from Funchal by taxi,
or by buses 20 or 21.
The most exhilarating
way, however, is to
go up by cable car
(from the station in
Funchal's Old Town)
and return by the
traditional Monte
toboggan . . . or you
can descend on foot;
the Caminho do
Monte is a steep but
direct road into
Funchal, passing
through some attrac-
tive older suburbs of
the city. To get onto
it, just follow the
toboggan run.

• Map H5
• Nossa Senhora do
Monte Church. 291 783
877. Open 9am–6pm
Mon–Sat, 8am–1pm
Sun. Free
• Quinta Jardins do
Imperador. Camhino do
Pico. 291 780 460.
9:30am–5:30pm
Mon–Sat. Admission (to
garden only) €6 (children
€3; under 12s free)
• Toboggan run. Dawn to
dusk. Fare €10 per
person plus tips

Top 10 Features

1 Toboggan Run
2 Railway Terminus
3 Church Steps
4 Nossa Senhora do Monte
5 Quinta do Monte
6 Cable Car Station
7 Capela da Coneição
8 Fountain Square
9 Quinta Jardins do Imperador
10 Parque do Monte

1 Toboggan Run
Madeira's toboggans
are steered by smartly
dressed *carreiros* (toboggan drivers) in straw
boaters on the 2-km
(1-mile) trip from Monte
to Livra-mento.

2 Railway Terminus
Now a café, this
building situated 550 m
(1,804 ft) above sea level
was a funicular railway
station until 1943.

3 Church Steps
On the Feast of the
Assumption (15 August),
pilgrims climb on their
knees up the steep steps
to Monte's church to
pay homage to the
statue of the Virgin,
which they believe
was presented by th
Virgin herself when
she appeared to a
shepherd girl in the
15th century.

The entrance to Monte Palace Tropical Garden lies to the south o
Nossa Senhora do Monte, near the start point for the toboggan ru

4 Nossa Senhora do Monte

Our Lady of Monte was inaugurated in 1818, replacing a 15th-century chapel built by Adam Ferreira (the first person to be born on Madeira – along with his twin sister, Eve). The church houses the tomb of Emperor Charles I of Austria.

6 Cable Car Station

The cable car's sleek steel-and-glass terminus is the only modern building in Monte. Along its route up the wild João Gomes Valley, you can see examples of many protected species of native trees and flowers.

7 Capela da Coneição

The pretty 18th-century Chapel of Conception stands in a tree-shaded square at the eastern end of the village, near a *miradouro* (viewing point) with views over the João Gomes Valley.

9 Quinta Jardins do Imperador

Just south of Monte (first right going downhill toward Funchal) is the beautiful mansion where Charles I lived in exile. The romantic knot gardens and lake are slowly being restored to their former glory.

10 Parque do Monte

This public park was laid out in 1894 beneath the stone railway viaduct now draped in climbing *Monstera deliciosa* plants. Cobbled paths thread in and out of the arches into a valley full of hydrangeas, tree ferns and massed agapanthus.

5 Quinta do Monte

Recently converted into a fine hotel *(see p113)*, the 19th-century Quinta do Monte sits in beautiful terraced grounds, open to the public during daylight hours. At the heart of the garden is the Baroque chapel of the Quinta do Monte, and below is a pretty garden gazebo, now serving teas.

8 Fountain Square

Set in a natural amphitheatre shaded by giant plane trees, Monte's main square is beautifully paved with sea-rounded cobbles. The square is named after the marble *fonte* of 1897 *(left)*. In its back wall is a niche housing a statue of the Virgin of Monte – a copy of the one in the church.

Emperor Charles I (1887–1922)

Charles I was ruler of an empire stretching from Vienna to Budapest. When it collapsed with Austria's defeat in World War I, he fled into exile, choosing the tiny island of Madeira because of his fond memories of holidays spent here. His happiness was short-lived: arriving on the island in November 1921, he succumbed to pneumonia and died in April 1922. Following Pope John Paul II's decision to beatify him, pilgrims now regularly visit his tomb in Monte's church.

Left *Nativity*, detail Middle **Swan Lake** Right **Japanese Garden**

🔟 Monte Palace Tropical Garden

1 Ancient Olives
Ancient trees can be dated by their girth; the girth of the three ancient olive trees growing just inside the entrance to the garden is at least as great as their height. Probably planted in 300 BC by the Romans, they are part of a group of 40 ancient olive trees rescued from the Alentejo in Portugal when the huge Alqueva Dam (Europe's largest artificial lake) was built.

Monte Palace Tropical Garden

2 Tile Pictures
The 40 tile panels lining the main avenue depict scenes from Portuguese history, from the reign of Afonso Henriques, who took Lisbon from the Moors in 1147, to Madeiran autonomy within Portugal in 1976.

Painted tiles near Swan Lake

3 Belvedere
The balcony at the south-western corner of the garden overlooks the road down to Funchal frequented by Monte's traditional toboggans. The road is now covered in asphalt, and the drivers have to struggle to make the toboggans travel at any speed. There are plans to restore the original cobbles so that the ride can once again live up to its description by the writer Ernest Hemingway as "the most exhilarating ride in the world".

4 Elephant's Foot Trees
North of the café at the bottom of the garden, you will find the aptly-named elephant's foot trees from Mexico.

5 World's Tallest Jar
The *Guinness Book of Records* has officially recognized this 5.345-m- (17-ft-) tall jar decorated with ancient Egyptian hieroglyphs as the world's tallest.

6 Swan Lake
The jar stands alongside a small lake enlivened by ducks, swans and docile carp, as well as fountains and fern-filled grottoes. The walls are decorated with Art Deco tiles rescued from demolished buildings in Lisbon. One advertises Japanese-style parasols *(left)*, another wicker furniture and oriental carpets.

7 Madeiran Flora

To the left of the main path is an area devoted to plants indigenous to Madeira's *laurisilva* forest *(see p23)*, including the thornless *Ilex perado* (Madeiran holly) and *Euphorbia piscatoria* (known in Portuguese as *Figuera do inferno* – "the fig from hell"), whose poisonous sap was once used for stunning fish.

8 Limestone Nativity

On the terrace above the lake, look for the 16th-century *Nativity* carved in fine-grained limestone by the Renaissance artist Jean de Rouen. The panels depicting shepherds and their flocks are especially charming.

9 Tiles and Sculpture

The terraces are also decorated with 17th- and 18th-century tile "wainscots" painted with cherubs and religious scenes, salvaged from demolished convents and chapels around Portugal. Note, too, the fine Italian Romanesque well head, with its amusing motto, "The more you give, the less you have to worry about!"

10 Japanese Garden

Guarded by leonine marble temple dogs, the Japanese Garden's lush green vegetation contrasts sharply with the bright red of the gardens' bridges and traditional Japanese archways.

Top 10 Other Quintas to Visit

1. Quinta da Boa Vista
2. Quinta do Bom Sucesso
3. Quinta das Cruzes
4. Quinta do Furão
5. Quinta Jardins do Imperador
6. Quinta Magnólia
7. Quinta do Monte
8. Quinta do Palheiro Ferreiro
9. Quinta da Palmeira
10. Quinta Vigia

Monte Palace

Monte Palace was a more modest mansion in the 18th century, when the estate belonged to the English consul Charles Murray. Later expanded into a hotel, it now belongs to the José Berardo Foundation, an educational and environmental concern endowed by a Madeira-born entrepreneur who made his fortune extracting gold from mining waste in South Africa. The terraces around the house display ancient and modern sculptures, as well as peacocks and "Ali Baba" pots. ⊗ Camhino do Monte • Map H5 • 291 782 339 • Gardens: open 9:30am–6pm daily. Admission €10 (under 15s free)

Monte Palace

For more on the Quintas listed above **See pp14–15, 20, 24–5, 26, 27, 44–45, 56, 59**

Curral das Freiras

The easiest way to get a feel for the sublime grandeur of Madeira's mountainous interior is to visit Curral das Freiras ("Nuns' Refuge"), the hidden valley used as a hideaway by the nuns of Santa Clara Convent (see pp16–17) whenever pirates attacked the island. (The same name is also given to the little village that now nestles there.) From such a beautiful spot, they must have returned to their city convent with a heavy heart. Visiting in 1825, H N Coleridge (the nephew of the English poet) described the Curral as "one of the great sights of the world".

Nuns Valley Café, Curral das Freiras

At the Nuns Valley Café, coffee is served on a terrace with spectacular views.

Many tour companies in Funchal offer half-day trips to Curral das Freiras, often in combination with Monte *(see p26)* or Câmara de Lobos *(see p75)*. Most of these trips go only as far as Eira do Serrado, the viewing point above the village.

Curral das Freiras is on the route of Autocarros da Camacha bus 81.

• Map G4

Top 10 Features

1. Eira do Serrado
2. Miradouro
3. The Sublime
4. View to the East
5. View to the North
6. View to the West
7. Footpath
8. Road
9. Chestnut Woods
10. Village

1 Eira do Serrado

Admiring this vista from Eira do Serrado *(right)* is as much a part of a visit to Curral das Freiras as the descent into the village itself. There is a hotel and restaurant, so if you fall in love with the romantic view, you can stay for lunch or dinner, or even spend the night *(see p116)*.

2 Miradouro

From the car park in front of the hotel, a short footpath leads up to a *miradouro*, or viewing point *(below)*, high above the Socorridos Valley. From here, the village far below looks like "Shangri-La" – the utopia of James Hilton's novel *Lost Horizon* (1933).

3 The Sublime

To cater to the 18th- and early 19th-century taste for the "sublime" in art, painters of the time visiting Madeira would deliberately exaggerate the height of mountains and waterfalls.

4 View to the East

Because of its cauldron-like shape, early explorers thought the Curral das Freiras, with its dramatic cliffs rising sheer to the east, was a collapsed volcano. In fact, the circular form is purely the result of millions of years of river and rain erosion.

5 View to the North

To the north beyond the village, a road heads to the valley, currently ending just after it disappears from view. There are plans to tunnel through the island's mountainous centre and take the road to the north coast, endangering the tranquillity of the Curral.

6 View to the West

To the west is a serrated ridge with three prominent peaks: Pico do Cavalho, Pico do Serradhino and, highest of all at 1,654 m (5,427 ft), Pico Grande. Beyond, the next great valley runs from Ribeira Brava to São Vicente via the Encumeada Pass *(see p81)*.

7 Footpath

To prolong your visit to the Curral, you can walk down to the village along the cobbled footpath *(above)* that begins in the car park. The path has 52 bends; at the bottom, turn right and walk uphill to the village. You can return by bus 81.

8 Road

Until the road was built in 1959, the only way in and out of the valley was the footpath; but even the road is little more than a ledge cut into the cliff face, and with two stretches of tunnel, it cannot cope with big tour buses.

9 Chestnut Woods

The descent to the village takes you through chestnut woods *(left)*. The trees bear white, sweetly scented flower stems in August, and produce edible chestnuts in October. Lower down, there is natural *laurisilva* forest *(see p23)*. In June, look out for wild orchids.

Pirates Ahoy!

Pirates were a serious menace in the early history of Madeira, which is why Funchal has no less than three forts. The worst attack occurred in 1566, when the French pirate Bertrand de Montluc, landed at Praia Formosa with 1,000 men and plundered the city's churches and mansions over a 15-day period, massacring all who stood in their way. Montluc gained nothing from his piracy, as he died from a wound he received in the attack.

10 Village

The café owners will urge you to try their chestnut dishes *(right)* – roasted salted chestnuts, rich chestnut soup and sweet chestnut cake. Sample, too, the delicious chestnut liqueur *castanha*.

🔟 Pico do Arieiro

Mountaineering equipment is not needed to get to the top of Madeira's third highest peak, because a road takes you all the way from the bustle of Funchal to the silence of the summit in less than an hour. The mountain top provides a viewing platform from which to look out over the multiple peaks and ravines of the island's central mountains. Standing aloft here, you have chance to study the astonishing range of rock formations left over from the violent volcanic upheavals that led to the creation of the island.

The view from Pico do Arieiro

🍴 There is a convenient café at the summit.

📷 Pico do Arieiro can be wrapped in cloud for much of the day. The best times of day for fine weather are before 10am and after 5pm. Alternatively, you can take a chance on the clouds clearing for your visit. It is often possible to drive up through the clouds and emerge to find the summit basking in sunshine.

Even at the height of summer, it can be cold and windy at the summit, and in winter, ice and snow are common. It is best to take warm and waterproof clothing.

• Map G4

Top 10 Features

1. Ecological Park
2. Ice House
3. Sheep Pens
4. Trig Point
5. Footpath
6. Café
7. View to the West
8. Volcanic Dykes
9. View to the East
10. Wildlife

1 Ecological Park
Some 12 km (7 miles) out of Funchal on the drive up, you pass the entrance to the Ecological Park, where primeval forest is being restored. With its viewing points and glades, it is popular for picnics.

2 Ice House
This igloo-shaped building *(above)*, 2 km (1 mile) south of the peak, is called Poço da Neve ("Snow Well"), and was built in 1813 by an Italian ice cream maker. Ice from pits like this one provided wealthy hotel guests with "snow water" in the heat of summer.

3 Sheep Pens
Livestock has been banned from the Ecological Park to allow Madeiran bilberry and heather to thrive, but sheep and goats graze around the summit and their circular pens are seen here

4 Trig Point
A short scramble up from the café brings you to the actual summit, 1,818 m (5,965 ft) above sea level. It is marked by a concrete post used for measuring altitude and location *(below*

Buses do not go to the peak, but taxis will take you there and back for a fixed fee.

Footpath
5 A footpath *(right)* links four main peaks and is one of the island's most exciting walks. It should not

be attempted unless you are properly equipped for challenging mountain conditions (including sudden storms, tunnels and unprotected drops). A large yellow sign marks the start of the path. Walk the first 100 m (110 yards) or so for fine views back to the summit.

Café
6 The photographs on the walls of the summit café show the peak at sunset, at sunrise and in snow. They might well tempt you to make return visits to enjoy the colours of the sky at dusk or dawn, or to view the night sky away from the glare of city lights.

View to the West
7 The view westward from the summit *(above)* takes in the entire central mountain range, with its succession of knife-edge peaks as far as the eye can see. The predominant colours are the fiery reds, rust browns, blacks and purples of oxidized volcanic rocks, in a scene more like the surface of Mars than the Earth.

Volcanic Dykes
8 Another distinctive feature of the view to the west and south is a series of parallel grey outcrops, resembling the Great Wall of China, that follow the contours of the landscape. These are, in fact, vertical seams of hard volcanic rock that have resisted the erosive forces of rain, frost and wind.

View to the East
9 The view to the east looks down over the green wooded slopes of the island's indigenous forest *(see p23)*. On a clear day, it is possible to see the meadow landscape of Santo da Serra, and the island's long rocky tail, the Ponta de São Lourenço, curving off into the distance.

Wildlife
10 Even on the bare, dry rocks of Madeira's high peaks, plants find a niche wherever a crack provides shelter and moisture. Among the gorse *(right)* and heather, you can spot grasshoppers and the well-camouflaged native grayling butterfly.

Island Origins

Madeira's long, slow birth began 18 million years ago, as lava burst up through the ocean floor to create layer upon layer of basaltic rock. It took 15 million years for Pico do Arieiro to reach its present height. For another 2.25 million years, further eruptions spilled lava sideways from the island's central core, creating the flatter plains of the Paúl da Serra to the west and Santo da Serra to the east. Volcanic activity did not finally cease until 6,450 years ago, when the caves at São Vicente *(see p81)* were formed.

Left **Reid's Hotel** Right **Statue of Tristão Vaz Teixeira in Machico**

:10 Moments in History

1 Island Formation
Twenty million years ago the islands of the Madeiran group began to emerge from the sea (first Porto Santo, then Madeira and the Ilhas Desertas). Pockets of fertile soil were created as storms eroded the softer layers of volcanic ash. Slowly the island came to life, as seeds excreted by visiting birds took root and spread.

2 Early Visitors
Sailors visited Madeira to gather sap from dragon trees for use in dying clothes. Mentioned in the *Natural History* of Pliny the Elder (AD 23–79), Madeira first appears on the Medici Map of 1351, as "Isola de Lolegname" ("Wooded Isle").

3 Zarco Arrives
Prince Henry "the Navigator" (1394–1460), third son of King John I of Portugal, realized how valuable Madeira was to sailors exploring the Atlantic Ocean. He sent João Gonçalves Zarco (1387–1467) *(see p15)* to the islands. Zarco landed on Porto Santo, and returned in 1420 to claim Madeira for Portugal.

4 Colonization
Portuguese colonization of Madeira began in 1425, when Zarco returned to govern the southwestern half from Funchal. Tristão Vaz Teixeira controlled the northeastern half, and Bartolomeu Perestrelo governed Porto Santo. Machico was initially the capital, but Funchal had a better harbour and gained city status in 1508.

5 Prosperity
By 1470, Madeira's early settlers were exporting wheat, dyestuffs, wine and timber, but sugar produced the biggest profits. Trading with London, Antwerp, Venice and Genoa, the island bloomed for 150 years as Europe's main sugar producer, channelling the profits into building and art.

6 Wine
Quick profits and wealth became a thing of the past once Caribbean and Brazilian sugar hit European markets in the mid-16th century. *Malvazia* (Malmsey), a rich sweet wine, then took over as Madeira's main export. It is the favourite drink of Shakespeare's roistering character Falstaff.

Prince Henry "The Navigator"

7 The British Arrive
British merchants dominated the wine trade after Charles II married the Portuguese princess Catherine of Braganza in 1662, and British (and American) taxes on Madeira wine were reduced as part of the marriage settlement. So valuable was Madeira to the British that an armed force was sent in 1801 to prevent Napoleon from capturing it.

Preceding pages **Traditional A-framed houses, Santana**

8 Reid's Hotel

Once the Napoleonic Wars were over, Madeira became a popular winter holiday destination for those wealthy enough to afford to escape from northern Europe. Symbolic of the era is Reid's Hotel, founded by William Reid, who arrived a poor sailor in 1836 and made a fortune renting houses to aristocratic visitors.

9 Autonomy

Madeira escaped the worst effects of the two World Wars, but by 1974, the year of Portugal's Carnation Revolution, it had become Europe's poorest region. In that year, Portugal's dictatorship was toppled in a coup by army officers. Later, celebrating soldiers had carnations stuck in their gun barrels by joyous civilians. In 1976, Madeira became autonomous, except for tax, foreign policy and defence.

10 Investment

Funchal is nearing its 500th anniversary as the capital of an increasingly prosperous island. New harbours and roads have boosted tourism, as well as improving the transport of fresh produce. Its forests are protected as a UNESCO World Natural Heritage Site, and whales and dolphins have returned to its waters.

Catherine of Braganza

Top 10 Famous Visitors

1 Robert Machin
This shipwrecked sailor and his lover Anne of Hertford died on Madeira in the 1370s.

2 King Ladislaw III
Having lost the Battle of Varna in 1414, the former king of Poland was one of Madeira's first settlers.

3 Columbus
Columbus came as a sugar merchant in 1478–9, and returned in 1498 on his way to the New World for the last time.

4 Captain Kidd
Nobody has ever found the treasure that the pirate Captain Kidd is said to have buried on Ilhas Desertas in the 1690s.

5 Captain James Cook
The explorer called in at Madeira on his ship, the *Endeavour*, in 1768.

6 Napoleon
The vanquished French emperor bought wine at Funchal on his way to exile on St Helena in 1815.

7 Emperor Charles I
The last Austro-Hungarian emperor died in exile on Madeira in 1922 *(see p27)*.

8 George Bernard Shaw
Visiting in 1927, the Irish playwright praised his dancing instructor as "the only man who ever taught me anything".

9 Winston Churchill
Churchill wrote *The Hinge of Fate* (volume 4 of his memoirs) while staying at Reid's Hotel in 1949.

10 Margaret Thatcher
The future British prime minister, Margaret Thatcher, spent her honeymoon at the Savoy Hotel in 1951.

Left **Museu Photographia Vincentes** Right **Casa Museu Frederico de Freitas**

TOP 10 Museums

1 Museu de Arte Sacra, Funchal

Funchal's Religious Art Museum is renowned for its colourful 16th-century Flemish paintings, but also has many remarkable polychrome wooden statues *(see pp10–11)*.

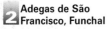

Franciscan saints, Museu de Arte Sacra

2 Adegas de São Francisco, Funchal

A guided visit to this charming, cobblestoned vintage Madeira wine lodge is a heady experience involving all the senses *(see pp12–13)*.

3 Museu da Quinta das Cruzes, Funchal

This is the house where Madeira's first ruler lived when Madeira was still young – the newest addition to Portugal's growing portfolio of overseas colonies at the start of the great Age of Discovery in the 15th century. Paintings and sketches of the island's major landmarks hang on the walls of the Quinta's richly decorated rooms *(see pp14–15)*.

Picnic by T. da Anunciacao, Museu da Quinta das Cruzes

4 A Cidade do Açúcar, Funchal

Devoted to the island's early sugar trade, this museum is also on the site of a house where Christophe Columbus stayed for six days in 1498, during his third voyage to the New World. ⊗ *Praça do Colombo 5 • Map P3 • 291 236 910 • 10am–12:30pm, 2–6pm Mon–Fri • Adm charge*

5 Museu Photographia Vicentes, Funchal

Founded by Vincent Gomes da Silva in 1852 (12 years after photography was invented), this photographic studio survives, complete with cameras, sets and costumes. ⊗ *Rua da Carreira 43 • Map P3 • 291 225 050 • 10am–12:30pm, 2–5pm Mon–Fri • Adm charge*

6 Museu Municipal e Aquário, Funchal

This museum offers a darkened aquarium downstairs, and a study collection of stuffed fish, birds and other Madeiran wildlife upstairs. ⊗ *Rua da Mouraria 33 • Map P2 • 291 229 761 • 10am–6pm Tue–Fri, noon–6pm Sat–Sun • Adm charge*

7 Casa Museu Frederico de Freitas, Funchal

Housed in a 19th-century mansion packed with antiques and religious paintings, this museum also has an amusing collection of teapots from all over the world. A new wing is devoted to ceramic tiles, with superb early examples from long-gone Madeiran churches. 🔖 *Calçada de Santa Clara 7 • Map N2 • 291 220 578 • 10am–12:30pm, 2–5:30pm Tue–Sat, 10am–12:30pm Sun • Adm charge*

8 Museu Henrique e Francisco Franco, Funchal

The artistic Franco brothers, painter Henrique (1883–1961) and sculptor Francisco (1855–1955), left Madeira to find fame in Lisbon and Paris. Their achievements are celebrated here. 🔖 *Rua João de Deus 13 • Map N4 • 291 230 633 • 10am–12:30pm, 2–6pm Mon–Fri • Adm charge*

Museu Henrique e Francisco Franco

9 Museu Etnográfico da Madeira, Ribeira Brava

A fascinating record of traditional life on Madeira. 🔖 *Rua de São Francisco 24 • Map D5 • 291 952 598 • 10am–12:30pm, 2–6pm Tue–Sun • Adm charge*

10 Museu da Baleia, Caniçal

Uplifting displays on the lives, history and conservation of the whale and other sea mammals. 🔖 *Largo Manuel Alves • Map L4 • 291 961 407 • 10am–noon, 1–6pm Tue–Sun • Adm charge (children free)*

Top 10 Museum Exhibits

1 Processional Cross
Superb Renaissance silverwork, with the Evangelists and biblical scenes in relief (Museu de Arte Sacra) *(see p10)*.

2 Max Romer Murals
Grape-harvest scenes capturing the vigour of youth and the golden light of autumn (Adegas de São Francisco) *(see p12)*.

3 Indian Miniature
The Virgin depicted as a Mogul princess (Room 1, Quinta das Cruzes) *(see p14)*.

4 Animal Bones
Bones that could have been chewed by Columbus, dug up by archaeologists (A Cidade do Açúcar).

5 Photo Albums
Sepia-tinted prints of 150 years of island life (Museu Photographia Vicentes).

6 Moray Eels
Sharp-fanged denizens of the deep (Museu Municipal e Aquário).

7 Winter Garden
Fern-filled, Art Nouveau glass conservatory at the Casa Museu Frederico de Freitas.

8 Boy with Cockerel
This portrait of a Madeiran peasant boy is one of Henrique Franco's best (Museu Henrique e Francisco Franco).

9 Fishing Boats
Boats painted blue, red, yellow and white were once common in every Madeiran fishing port (Museu Etnográfico da Madeira).

10 Scrimshaws
Whalebones carved and etched in the days before hunting whales was illegal (Museu da Baleia).

Left *Last Supper*, São Salvador Right **Funchal Cathedral (Sé)**

🔟 Churches

1 Funchal Cathedral (Sé)

Funchal cathedral set the pattern for the island's other churches with its *talha dourada* ("gilded woodwork"), as the Holy Sacrament chapel (to the right of the high altar) demonstrates (*see pp8–9*).

2 Santa Clara, Funchal

Founded in 1476 by João Gonçalves de Câmara, son of Zarco (*see pp15, 36*), this convent has changed little since it was first built (*see pp16–17*).

3 Igreja do Colégio, Funchal

The Jesuits, a brotherhood of missionary priests, owned large wine estates on Madeira, and spent some of their wealth on this lovely church, covered from floor to ceiling in frescoes, gilded carvings and rare ceramic tiles. The school they built alongside is now the University of Madeira.
🕙 *Praça do Município • Map P3*

Igreja do Colégio, Funchal

4 Igreja do São Pedro, Funchal

The main church until the cathedral was built, St Peter's has a wealth of gilded wood-work, some dating from the 17th century. The corn and grapes being gathered by angels in the right-hand chapel are symbolic of the bread and wine of Christ's Last Supper. A simple slab covers the grave of João de Mourarolim (died 1661), who paid for the decoration.
🕙 *Rua do São Pedro • Map N2*

5 São Salvador, Santa Cruz

This Gothic parish church was completed in 1512, when the tomb of the merchant Micer João, supported by crouching lions, was installed on the north side. Next to it is the chapel of the Morais family (1522). The altar has 16th-century paintings of the *Life of Christ* by Gregório Lopes, and the sacristy, entered through a Manueline portal, has a 16th-century carved and painted *Last Supper* tableau. 🕙 *Map K5*

6 Igreja da Nossa Senhora da Conceição, Machico

Probably designed by Pêro Anes, who designed Funchal cathedral, this church dates from 1499 and is noted for its south door – the white marble pillars come from Seville and were a gift from King Manuel I (1495–1521). So, too, was the statue of the Virgin kept in its tabernacle at the peak of the elaborately gilded high altar.
🕙 *Map K4*

Many churches in Funchal are open from 8am–noon or 1pm, then from 4–7:30pm. Others only open for services (around 8am, 6pm)

7 Capela dos Milagres, Machico

The Chapel of the Miracles takes its name from the 15th-century Flemish crucifix on the high altar. It was miraculously found floating at sea, years after the old chapel was washed away by a flood in 1803. The original chapel is said to have been built over the grave of Anne of Hertford and Robert Machin, legendary lovers shipwrecked here in the 14th century. ◈ Map K4

8 São Bento, Ribeira Brava

A lion and a basilisk (whose stare was said to turn humans to stone) are among the carvings on the capitals, font and pulpit of this Gothic parish church. Don't miss the magnificent 16th-century Flemish *Nativity* and statue of the Virgin. ◈ Map D5

Senhora da Luz, Ponta do Sol

9 Senhora da Luz, Ponta do Sol

Founded in 1486 by Rodrigo Anes, one of the first men granted land on Madeira by the Portuguese king, this lovely church has an original knotwork ceiling, a 16th-century Flemish altarpiece, and a unique ceramic font, glazed with green copper oxide to resemble bronze. ◈ Map D5

10 Capela do Loreto, Loreto

Another unspoiled, historic early church, boasting a knotwork ceiling and Gothic doorways of imported white marble. ◈ Map C4

Top 10 Religious Figures

1 St Laurence
São Lourenço was the name of the ship in which Captain Zarco (*see p36*) set sail for Madeira in 1420.

2 St Vincent
The patron saint of Portugal and of wine makers is depicted on the ceiling of the church in São Vicente (*see p81*).

3 Our Lady of Monte
According to local legend, the Virgin gave this statue to a shepherdess (*see p26*).

4 Our Lady of Terreiro da Luta
This huge statue (*see p78*) was built in thanks for protection during World War I.

5 St Anthony of Padua
The Lisbon-born saint preaches to fish in the Sacred Art Museum (*see p10*) and the Fishermen's Chapel (*see p42*).

6 St Ignatius Loyola
The founder of the Jesuit order graces the façade of the Colégio (*see p40*).

7 Christ the Redeemer
Erected in 1927, this clifftop statue (*see p87*) resembles the famous landmark in Brazil's capital, Rio de Janeiro.

8 St Francis and St Clare
Patron saints of Madeira's religious houses, the Santa Clara Convent (*see p16*) and the São Francisco Friary (*see p12*).

9 Mary Jane Wilson
Indian-born founder of a Madeira-based teaching order. ◈ *Wilson Museum: Rua do Carmo 61. Open 10am–noon, 3–5pm Tue–Sat, 10–noon Sun*

10 Emperor Charles I
Former Austrian emperor, buried in Monte (*see p26*) and beatified by Pope John Paul II.

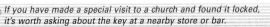

If you have made a special visit to a church and found it locked, it's worth asking about the key at a nearby store or bar.

Left **Câmara Municipal** Right **House of the Consuls**

Historic Buildings

1 Alfândega, Funchal

Designed in 1508 by Pêro Anes (who also designed the cathedral), the Customs House was built to collect the taxes levied by the Portuguese Crown on Madeira's timber, corn and sugar exports. Now home to the island's Regional Assembly, it has three splendid upper-floor rooms (*see p9*). ◈ *Rua da Alfândega • Map P3 • 291 210 500 • By appointment • Free*

2 Câmara Municipal, Funchal

Madeira's early 19th-century town hall originally belonged to the Count of Carvalhal (*see p24*). Look in the inner courtyard to see graceful balconies and a sensuous statue of *Leda and the Swan* (1880), brought here when the market was built in 1937 (*see p18*). ◈ *Praça do Município • Map N3 • Ask the porter for permission to view the courtyard*

Manueline door, Alfândega (Customs House)

3 Tower House, Funchal

Opposite the Museum of Sacred Art (*see pp10–11*) is a stately building with a *torre-mirante*. Typical of the grander of Funchal's town houses, these towers were built so the owners could view incoming ships. Note that the door handles are made from large iron keys. ◈ *Rua do Bispo • Map P3*

4 House of the Consuls, Funchal

Few traditional Madeiran houses are more ornate than this 18th-century house built for foreign diplomats. ◈ *Rua de Conceição • Map P3 • Closed to the public.*

5 Fishermen's Chapel, Câmara de Lobos

This simple, moving chapel on the harbour is where fishermen come to pray before and after they put out to sea. Wall paintings depict the story of how St Anthony of Padua (who was born in Lisbon) survived a shipwreck, and was so eloquent that even the fishes of the sea came to hear him preach. ◈ *Câmara de Lobos • Map F6*

6 Igreja Inglesa, Funchal

The English Church (1822) is a domed Neo-Classical building set in a delightful garden. Its construction was funded by public appeal; Nelson, George II and the Duke of Wellington all contributed. ◈ *Rua do Quebra Costas • Map P2*

7 Capela de Santa Catarina, Funchal

Founded in 1425 by Constança de Almeida, Zarco's wife, this chapel perched above the harbour, was the first to be built in Funchal. ◈ *Jardim de Santa Catarina • Map Q2*

Gold coins paid by the exiled Napoleon for a barrel of Madeira wine are buried beneath the foundation stone of the English Church.

Madeira University, Funchal

he 17th-century buildings of
is old Jesuit college are being
stored to form a new campus.
om the inner courtyard, there
e good views of the tower of
e Igreja do Colégio (*see p40*).
Rua dos Ferreiros • Map P3

Capela do Corpo Santo, Funchal

his 16th-century chapel in the
ona Velha (Old Town) was built
nd run by the Guild of São Pedro
onçalves, a self-help charity
hich raised funds for fishermen
nd their families. ⊗ *Rua Dom
arlos I • Map P5*

Banco de Portugal, Funchal

The Bank of Portugal building
940) maintains continuity with
aditional architecture, with its
obe-topped corner turret,
recian marble statues, and
uit-filled baskets symbolizing
ealth and plenty. Nearby, don't
iss Francisco Franco's *Zarco
Monument* (1927), showing
unchal's founder looking out to
ea. ⊗ *Avenida Zarco • Map P3*

anco de Portugal

Top 10 Flamboyant Buildings in Funchal

1 Toyota Car Showroom
The former Chamber of
Commerce on Avenida Arriaga
is clad in 1930s tile pictures
of Madeiran transport.

2 New Chamber of Commerce
Today's Chamber of Commerce
is located in a 15th-century
building off Rua dos Aranhas.

3 Pátio
The inner courtyard of the
1860s Pátio (Rua da Carreira
43) features a sweeping double
staircase leading to the
Vicentes Museum (*see p38*).

4 Rua da Carreira
A street of flamboyant iron
balconies – especially at
numbers 77–91 and 155.

5 Rua da Mouraria
Funchal's antiques quarter
has many aristocratic town
houses, including the Museu
Municipal (*see p38*).

6 Garden Gazebo
Take tea, admire the views
and watch the world go by at
a *casinha de prazer* ("pleasure
house") like the one in the
Freitas Museum (*see p38*).

7 Quintas
Ornate mansions like the
Quinta Palmeira (*see p45*) line
the terraces above Funchal.

8 Casino
The 1970s casino on
Avenida do Infante looks
wonderful lit up at night.

9 Apartamentos Navio Azul
Reminiscent of an ocean liner,
this 1970s block stands beside
the Estrada Monumental.

10 Madeira Cable Car Station
Funchal's newest public building
is a futuristic cube of steel
and glass on Rua Dom Carlos.

Left **Jardim Botânico (Botanical Gardens), Funchal** Right **Quinta do Palheiro Ferreiro**

🔟 Gardens

1 Jardim de São Francisco, Funchal

St Francis, the patron saint of the environment, would firmly approve of this richly planted garden, built in the city centre on the site of Funchal's long-gone Franciscan friary. It is only the size of a city block, but so full of scented and flowering plants, shaded by some truly enormous trees, that you could be in the middle of the jungle. ⬡ *Avenida Arriaga • Map P2 • Free*

2 Jardim de Santa Catarina, Funchal

On the walk from downtown to the hotel zone, this terraced park has fantastic views over the harbour. Look out for statues of Henry the Navigator at the lower end, Christopher Columbus by the Capela de Santa Catarina *(see p42)* and Francisco Franco's *Semeador* (the "Sower," 1919, *see p39*), symbolically throwing handfuls of seed across the grass. ⬡ *Avenida do Infante • Map Q2 • Free*

3 Quinta das Cruzes, Funchal

The flower-filled grounds of this "archaeological park" *(see p14)* boasts grave slabs, a private chapel, a wonderful orchid garden and a *casinha de prazer* ("pleasure house"), perched on the walls to take advantage of the views *(see pp14–15)*.

Carved lions in Quinta das Cruzes

Monte Palace Tropical Garden

4 Monte Palace Tropical Garden, Monte

This intriguing botanical garden full of caves, fountains, lakes, fish ponds, Japanese temples, stone and bronze sculptures, and nove tile pictures *(see pp28–9)*.

5 Quinta Magnólia, Funchal

The Quinta Magnólia, built the 1820s as home to the US consul, now houses the Foreign Culture Library. Its palm-filled gardens (with public pool, tennis courts an playground) lie along the terraced flanks o the Ribeira Seca valle ⬡ *Rua do Dr Pita • 9am–du Mon–Fri • Map G6 • Free*

6 Quinta Vigia, Funchal

The lovingly maintained official gardens of Madeira's president are open on weekday provided that no official functior are taking place. ⬡ *Avenida do Infante • Map Q1 • Free*

7 Quinta do Palheiro Ferreiro, Palheiro Ferreiro
Subtropical plants in unusual and imaginative combinations are displayed in a style that is recognizably English *(see pp24–5)*.

8 Jardim Botânico, Funchal
These extraordinary gardens are a showcase for Madeira's varied plant life *(see pp20–21)*.

9 Hospício Princesa Dona Maria Amélia, Funchal
Popular for wedding photos, this hospital was founded in memory of Brazilian princess Maria Amélia, who died here in 1853. ◈ *Avenida do Infante • Map Q1 • Free*

10 Quinta Palmeira, Funchal
Despite being blighted by one of Funchal's new fast highways, this former home of the Gordon wine family hovers between garden and wilderness, with manicured rose gardens, tiled fountains, and grottoes and jungle-like areas yet to be restored. Don't miss the 15th-century Columbus Window, rescued from the home of João Esmeraldo. ◈ *Rua da Levada de Santa Luzia 31A • Map P5 • 291 221 091 • 9am–noon, 2–5pm Mon–Fri • Adm charge*

Columbus Window, Quinta Palmeira

Top 10 Madeiran Plants and Flowers

1 King Protea
These South African plants, similar to giant artichokes, are in demand for flower displays.

2 Slipper Orchid
Mainly flowering in the winter months, slipper orchids need jungle-like shade.

3 Mexican Poinsettia
These festive plants bloom right on cue for Christmas; note that the showy, scarlet part is actually the bract, not the flower.

4 Aloe
Fleshy leaves edged with spines produce flower spikes up to 1 m (3 ft) high. The sap is harvested, and used in making aloe vera skin products.

5 Agapanthus
The blue-and-white globe-shaped blossoms of the Lily of the Nile line Madeira's roadside banks in summer.

6 Strelitzia
Is it a bird or is it a plant? These long-lived flowers look like exotic birds of paradise.

7 Angel's Trumpet
White, yellow or amber, the datura's long trumpets both smell and look beautiful.

8 Arum Lily
Pure white and sweetly scented, these flowers symbolize the Virgin Mary and virginity.

9 Flame of the Forest
Crowned by orange-red coxcombs, these trees are descended from seed brought to Madeira by Captain Cook in 1772.

10 Jacaranda
Funchal's Avenida Arriaga turns into a river of blue when these striking Brazilian trees flower in spring.

Left **Beach at Praia Formosa** Right **Rock pools, Porto Moniz**

🔟 Beaches

1 Praia Formosa
Steep-sided Madeira does not have many beaches – cliffs and rocky shores are the norm – so Praia Formosa ("Beautiful Beach"), a stretch of grey, sea-smoothed pebbles between Funchal and Câmara de Lobos, is a notable exception. Madeira's government has just begun to realize what an asset this could be; it has plans to landscape the area around the beach and remove the unsightly oil depots. ◈ *Map G6*

Câmara de Lobos

2 Câmara de Lobos
Madeira's most photogenic beach was put on the map when Winston Churchill, the famous British wartime prime minister, set up his easel here in 1949. Churchill was an accomplished artist, with an eye for a well-composed scene. Nearly 50 years later, that scene has not changed: colourfully striped fishing boats are still lined up on the cobbles of the little beach for cleaning and repair. ◈ *Map G6*

3 Ponta do Sol
The beach at Ponta do Sol ("Sun Point") is the perfect place to watch the setting sun. Dramatic clouds float like islands in a pink and purple sky. ◈ *Map D5*

4 Jardim do Mar
In October, the narrow strip of west-facing rocky beach connecting Jardim do Mar and Paúl do Mar is the point from which surfers gain access to the waves. Surfers need to bring their own equipment as there are no rental facilities. ◈ *Map B4*

5 Porto Moniz
Thundering waves dash Madeira's northern shores along the dramatic north coast road to Porto Moniz, but once there you can relax in the sun-warmed water of natural rock pools, and let those same waves shower you with spray. ◈ *Map B1*

6 São Jorge
About 2 km (1 mile) east of São Jorge, a sign to *Praia* ("Beach") directs you to the estuary of the São Jorge river, where you can either swim in a natural pool in the bend of the river or, if you prefer, in the sea (access is from the small pebble beach). There's a beach café selling drinks and snacks. ◈ *Map*

7 Prainha
A pretty, sheltered bay with a beachside café at its eastern end, Prainha has Madeira's only

naturally sandy beach. (Calheta, on the south coast, now also has a sandy beach – created with sand imported from Morocco.) ⊗ Map L4

8 Garajau and Caniço
A path from the statue of Christ the Redeemer at Garajau winds down to a beach popular for snorkelling and diving. It marks the start of a marine reserve with underwater caves leading to Caniço de Baixo, which can also be reached from the Lido at the Hotel Galomar (see p49). ⊗ Map J6

9 Praia dos Reis Magos
Continuing eastward from Caniço de Baixo, a new seafront promenade leads to Praia dos Reis Magos, a rocky beach with a scatter of fishermen's huts and a couple of simple cafés selling freshly grilled fish – idyllic for crowd-shy romantics. ⊗ Map J6

10 Porto Santo
If a holiday is incomplete for you without basking on a sandy beach, then take a ferry or a flight (see p103) to Porto Santo, 40 km (25 miles) north-east of Madeira, where you can enjoy a 10-km (6-mile) stretch of unspoilt golden sand (see p95). ⊗ Map L2

Long sandy beach, Porto Santo

Top 10 Swimming Pools

1 Savoy Resort
The biggest and best of all the hotel pools (see p112).

2 Reid's
Close competitor to the Savoy, shaded by palms in a garden setting (see p112).

3 Quinta Magnólia
Once exclusive to the British Country Club, now open to all (see p44).

4 Lido
The island's biggest leisure pool complex, with access to the sea. ⊗ Rua do Gorgulho • Map G6 • 8:30am–8pm daily

5 Clube Naval
Upmarket version of the Lido, 1 km (half a mile) further west around the promenade. ⊗ Map G6 • 10am–6pm daily

6 Ponta Gorda
In the next bay west of the Clube Naval, perfect for toddlers and sea access. ⊗ Map G6 • 10am–6pm daily

7 Complexo Balnear de Barreirinha
Just east of the Fortaleza de São Tiago; a small pool but good diving platform and sea access. ⊗ Rua de Santa Maria • Map Q6 • 10am–6pm daily

8 Santa Cruz Lido
A mini-Miami; small Art Deco lido with swimming and paddling pools, sea access, and views of landing aircraft. ⊗ Map K5 • 10am–6pm daily

9 Porto da Cruz
Natural rock pools with concrete extensions; enjoy luxuriating in sun-warmed sea water dashed by sea spray. ⊗ Map J3

10 Caniçal
A spanking new lido with café on the western side of the harbour. ⊗ Map L4

Left **Diving** Right **Golf**

🔟 Outdoor Activities

1 Helicopter Ride
A 15-minute helicopter trip around Madeira's valleys and canyons will give you that James Bond feeling and show you the island from a different point of view. It isn't cheap, but it's certainly memorable. 🔗 *HeliAtlântis, Estrada da Pontinha, Funchal Container Port • Map Q2 • 291 232 882*

Panoramic Balloon

2 Panoramic Balloon
Another way to gain an aerial perspective on Funchal is to float above the city in a basket dangling from the underside of the world's largest gas-filled balloon. The globe, 20 m (66ft) high, takes up to 30 passengers 150 m (492 ft) into the sky, descending to the beach again by means of an electric winch. 🔗 *The Madeira Balloon, Avenida do Mar • Map Q3 • 291 282 700 • Trips every 15 minutes from 9am–10:30pm daily • Adm charge*

3 Boat Trips
Booths located around Funchal's marina have details of all the cruising options available, from day-long trips to Ilhas Desertas (see p88) and half-day whale- and dolphin-watching tour to shorter sunset cruises. 🔗 *Funchal Marina • Map Q3 • Albatroz: 291 223 36 • Bonita da Madeira: 291 762 218*

4 Deep-sea Fishing
Fishing trips can be booked around the marina. A tag-and-release policy ensures fish are released into the wild once caugh (see p106). 🔗 *Funchal Marina • Map C • Turipesca: 291 231 063 • Balancal: 291 794 901 • Nautisantos: 291 231 312*

5 Walking
With more than 1,600 km (994 miles) of rural footpaths to choose from, it's no wonder tha thousands of people visit every year just to walk in the island's mountains and forests (see p50

6 Tennis
Madeira's five-star hotels have their own courts, but you can also play on the public court in the Quinta Magnólia. Booking are made at the gatekeeper's lodge at the entrance. 🔗 *Rua do Dr Pita • Map G6*

7 Golf
Two of Europe's most scen courses are located in the east of the island at Santo da Serra and Palheiro Ferreira. Transport can be arranged from Funchal, and equipment hired. 🔗 *Clube de Golfe de Santo da Serra: Map K4. 550 10 • Palheiro Golf: Sítio do Balancal, São Gonçalo. Map J5. 291 790 120*

Diving

Clean Atlantic waters, clear visibility and an array of beautiful fish and reefs make Madeira a popular spot for divers of all ages and abilities. ◈ *Manta Diving Center, Hotel Galomar, Caniço de Baixo. Map J6. 291 935 588 • Madeira Divepoint, Hilton Madeira Hotel, Largo Antonio Nobre, Funchal. Map H6. 291 239 579*

Adventure Sports

Madeira's challenging countryside lends itself to all sorts of adventure sports, from rock-climbing to hang-gliding, but few companies yet exist to provide organized excursions. One that does is Terras de Aventura, offering mountain biking, jeep safaris, off-road walking, climbing, kayaking, canyoning and paragliding. ◈ *291 776 818 • www.terrasdeaventura.com*

Horse Riding

The Associação Hípica da Madeira can provide lessons for beginners; for more experienced riders there are guided tours along Madeira's beautiful, narrow mountain tracks and hidden forest byways. ◈ *Quinta Vila Alpires, Caminho dos Pretos, São João de Latrão. Map H5 • 291 792 582 • Open 3–6pm Tue, 10am–1pm, 3–6pm Wed–Sun (Sun to 7pm)*

Horse riding

Top 10 Madeiran Wildlife

1 Wall Lizards
You will see them on every sunny rock or pavement. They feed on fruit and flies.

2 Wagtails
This yellow-breasted bird is never very far from water, hence its Madeiran nickname: "the washerwoman".

3 Swifts
Watch them wheeling and feeding at dusk along Funchal's seafront promenade.

4 Kestrels
These chestnut-backed birds nest on the cliffs of the hotel district, and hover on the wind in search of prey.

5 Buzzards
Often seen riding the warm air above the valleys of Funchal and Curral das Freiras.

6 Robins
The robins you will see on Madeira have the same cheery red breasts as their mainland cousins, and just as sweet a song.

7 Sally Lightfoot Crabs
These dark brown crabs are often seen grazing tidal rocks for algae. They will disappear fast if threatened – hence "lightfoot".

8 Perez's Frogs
Introduced to Madeira by the Count of Carvalhal, this noisy frog with a bright yellow backbone stripe has spread to every pond in the island.

9 Monarch butterflies
These large orange-black-and-white gliding butterflies are seen in all Madeiran gardens.

10 Limpets
Limpets are a traditional food on Madeira, but harvesting is now controlled to prevent over-exploitation.

Left **Walkers at Rabaçal** Right **Water feeding a *levada***

Facts about Levada Walking

1 What Are Levadas?
The word *levada* means "to take". A *levada* is an irrigation channel, designed to take water from places where it is plentiful to those where it is not. The Madeirans borrowed the idea from the mountains of Andalucia, where the channels are known as *acequias*.

2 Why Levadas were Built
Water is abundant in the mountains to the north of the island, but scarce in the fertile and sunny south, where most crops are grown. Looking for a way to store water and carry it to their cultivation terraces and fields, the island's early settlers began to build the irrigation channels that form the basis of today's network.

3 Water and Power
Water was essential to the growth of Madeira. It irrigated

Terracing

the wheat, sugar, grape and banana crops, powered the sawmills used to turn trees into timber for construction and ship building, and turned the wheels the mills that crushed sugar.

4 Levada Maintenance
Levadas require constant maintenance to remove rockfall and vegetation that could block the flow of water. Paths were constructed alongside the channels to allow the *levadeiro* or maintenance man, to patrol his length of *levada* and keep it in good working order.

5 Levadas as Footpaths
On a visit to Madeira in 19?? Pat and John Underwood realiz?? that *levada* maintenance paths made perfect footpaths – many which provide the visitor with ea?? walking routes, with spectacula?? views. The resulting guide book?? *Landscapes of Madeira* (Sunflow?? Books), has brought thousands walkers to the island.

6 Construction
Constructing *levadas* was a feat of engineering. Following the contours meant digging channels into the face of sheer cliffs, or building aqueducts ove?? deep crevices. To reach inacces?? ible spots, *levada* builders were lowered down cliffs in baskets.

7 Contour Lines
To prevent the water from running too fast, causing soil

rosion, most *levadas* follow the
ontours of the landscape, wind-
g in and out of valleys,
escending gradually from the
igh peaks of the island's central
hassif to the ridges and terraces
f the south.

8 Guided Tours

Levada walking is easiest if
ou join a guided tour. Madeira
xplorers and Nature Meetings
re good companies; the tourist
oard *(see p102)* will have details
f others. ● *Madeira Explorers. 219 763*
01 • Nature Meetings. 291 200 686

Waterfall, Risco Valley

9 Levada dos Tornos

You can combine a *levada*
valk with a visit to the Quinta do
alheiro Ferreiro *(see pp24–5).*
xit the garden, turn right, and
valk up to the village. Beyond the
afé, look for signs to the Levada
los Tornos and Jasmin Tea House
– an ideal spot for lunch *(see p79).*

10 Rabaçal

A popular walk, if you are
isiting the Paúl da Serra *(see*
82), starts from Rabaçal. From
here, walk down to the Foresters'
House, and turn right along the
evada signposted "Risco". After
20 to 30 minutes' walk through
primeval woodland you will reach
a pretty waterfall.

Top 10 Levada Tips

1 Sunflower Guide
Don't go anywhere
without an accurate map
and reliable directions.
Sunflower's *Landscapes of*
Madeira has both, and is
updated constantly.

2 Dimensions
A typical *levada* is 0.5 m
(one and a half ft) wide and 0.8
m (two and a half ft) deep, with
narrow paths 1 m (3 ft) wide.

3 How Far Can You Go?
There are now 2,200 km
(1,365 miles) of *levada* paths
to choose from – it would
take three consecutive
months to walk them all.

4 Footwear
Paths can be both muddy
and slippery, so be sure to
wear sensible weatherproof,
non-slip footwear.

5 Temperature
It can be cold and wet
higher up Madeira's moun-
tains, so take warm and
waterproof clothing.

6 Water
Water is everywhere, but
it is not fit to drink, so carry
your own supplies.

7 Tunnels
Carry a small light so that
you can negotiate tunnels
without bumping your head.

8 Vertigo
Some *levada* paths have
very steep drops. Turn back if
you experience dizziness.

9 Last Resort
If vertigo strikes, as a last
resort you can always get into
the *levada* channel and walk
to safety.

10 Vegetation
Levada paths pass trees
festooned with hair-like lichen,
and cliffs with beautiful and
succulent ferns.

Left **Caves at São Vincente** Right **Parrot Park, Funchal**

TOP 10 Children's Attractions

1 Grutas de São Vincente

These caves were created by molten rock. A cave tour, simulated eruptions and a short film will teach you about Madeira's volcanic origins. ◈ *São Vicente, Sítio do Pé do Passo* • *Map E2* • *291 842 404* • *Adm charge*

2 Santa Maria de Colombo

There are lots of boat trips to choose from *(see p48)*, but younger children will particularly enjoy a trip on a replica of the Santa Maria, the ship that took Columbus across the Atlantic. ◈ *Tickets from Marina do Funchal* • *Map Q3* • *291 220 327* • *Trips 10:30am–1:30pm, 3–6pm daily; twilight cruises Jun–Sep: 7:15–8:45pm* • *Adm charge*

3 Dolphin-watching

Few encounters with nature are as exciting as those with

Dolphin-watching

dolphins or whales in their natural habitat, but this trip will appeal more to older children, as a patient wait is not always met with an appearance. ◈ *Tickets from Marina do Funchal* • *Map Q3* • *Adm charge*

4 Football

Madeira has two soccer teams, Marítimo and Nacional; both play in the Portuguese First League. Home matches are friendly, family occasions. ◈ *Marítimo: Estádio dos Barreiros, Rua do D. Pita, Funchal. Map G6* • *Nacional: Choupana Stadium. Map H5* • *Adm charge*

5 Twin Peaks

There is something magical about emerging from the sun and looking across the peaks of Funchal from the Pico do Arieiro *(see p32)*, Madeira's third highest peak at 1,810 metres (5,938 ft). The 5-km (3-mile) round trip on foot to the top of Pico Ruivo, Madeira's highest peak at 1,862 m (6,109 ft) *(see p77)*, is within the capacity of fit children over the age of nine.

6 Ribeiro Frio

The trout farm at Ribeiro Frio is fun for younger children, as they can get close to fish at different stages of growth. The walk from Ribeiro Frio to Balcões *(see p51)* is safe for children as the *levada* is dry, so they will not get wet if they fall in. ◈ *Map H4*

Santa Maria de Colombo

Parrot Park
7 Depending on the age of your children, you can either let them enjoy the playful antics of parrots and parakeets, or engage them in discussion about the ethics of keeping wild creatures in cages for human amusement. While you're here, you can also explore the Botanical Garden *(see pp20–21).*

Monte Cable Car
8 The Monte cable car *(see p27)* is as good as a theme-park ride as you fly high over the João Gomes Valley. Once in Monte, you can explore the Palace Tropical Garden *(see pp28–9)*, where children under 14 get in free.

Trout farm, Ribeiro Frio

Shopping
9 If your children are mad about shopping, head for Madeira Shopping *(see p69)*, with its branded fashion outlets, fast food cafés, seven-screen cinema and bowling alley. ✆ *Cinemas Castello Lopes: 291 706 760*

Swimming
10 Toddlers have a pool just made for them at Ponta Gorda in the Hotel Zone, just west of the Club Navale. For older children and confident swimmers, the Lido complex, in the Hotel Zone, has a big pool, sunbathing decks and access to the ocean. ✆ *Map Q1*

Top 10 Tips for Families

Hotels
1 Stay in a five-star hotel for the extra facilities, such as pools, tennis, games rooms, mini-golf and satellite TV.

Indulgence
2 Madeirans love children, so yours will get plenty of friendly attention.

Downtown
3 You can safely let older children wander on their own; crime is almost non-existent.

Downtown Cinemas
4 The Anadia Shopping Centre opposite Funchal's main market *(see pp18–19)* has a two-screen cinema. ✆ *Map P4 • 291 207 040*

"Beatles" Boat
5 Moored in concrete on Avenida do Mar is a boat owned by the Beatles in 1966, a cool place for an ice cream.

Playgrounds
6 The best playgrounds in Funchal are in the grounds of Quinta Magnólia and Jardim de Santa Catarina *(see p44).*

Funchal Marina
7 Stroll around the marina to spot fish, boats and pictures painted on the concrete walls by visiting sailors. ✆ *Map Q3*

Promenade
8 Families stroll along Avenida do Mar and buy snacks from Turkish-style kiosks.

Porto Moniz
9 Known as "nature's pools", the rock pools at Port Moniz are great for bathing in warm, shallow water. ✆ *Map B1*

Porto Santo
10 Virtually traffic free, Porto Santo is a place to let your children off the leash to explore by bike or on foot.

Left **Madeira Carnival** Right **New Year**

TOP 10 Festivals

1 Christmas Cribs
The festive year begins in December when churches and shops mount cribs with a cast of traditional characters, including rustic shepherds. If you visit outside Christmas, you can see antique crib figures at the Quinta das Cruzes and the Casa Museu Frederico de Freitas *(see p38)*.

Flower Festival

2 New Year Lights
Colourful street lights are suspended across the main streets of Funchal from early December, but New Year is even more spectacular, as locals open their curtains and switch on their house and car lights, flooding Funchal's amphitheatre with light. Fireworks explode, ships blow their hooters, and cars their horns.

3 Carnival
Carnival is celebrated over three days before Shrove Tuesday. Schools, youth clubs and marching bands parade the streets in fancy dress, followed by the colourful allegorical parade that fills the city on the last day. Though not as wild as Rio, this carnival is still an excuse to let your hair down.

4 Flower Festival
Scarcely is Carnival over before the floats come out again for the spring Flower Festival in April. Originally created as a tourist attraction, this is a festival that Madeirans have now taken to their heart, with passionate competition among local clubs to produce the best float.

5 St James (São Tiago)
Funchal has its very own "village" festival on 1 May, when city dignitaries process up Rua de Santa Maria to the 18th-century Baroque Socorro church and place their chains of office at the feet of St James (Funchal's patron saint), renewing the city's pledge to honour him for rescuing them in 1523 from the plague.

6 Atlantic Festival
Held in late May and early June, the Festival do Atlântico combines fireworks, street entertainment and music festival. There are performances by international stars as well as the accomplished local musicians of the Orquestra Clássica da Madeira, the Orquestra de Mandolins and the Funchal Brass Ensemble.

7 Assumption in Monte
The Virgin is greatly revered by pious Madeirans because they believe she takes pity on human suffering. 15 August, the day on which she is believed to have been assumed into heaven, is observed in Monte *(see p26)*.

...th religious services and pro-
...ssions by day, and feasting,
...usic and dancing by night.

B Ponta Delgada
Another important religious
...stival is held in Ponta Delgada
...ee p78) on the first Sunday in
...eptember, when pilgrims from
...over the island come to pray
...the Bom Jesus ("Good Jesus"),
...figure of Christ believed to
...ve miraculous powers.

9 Wine Festival
In mid September, the grape
...rvest is celebrated in Estreito
...e Câmara de Lobos, with folk
...usic and demonstrations of
...ape-crushing done the old-
...shioned way – with bare feet.
...ere are also special wine-
...lated menus and events.

0 Nossa Senhora da Piedade
...e church on the hill above the
...each at Prainha in eastern
...adeira is locked for most of the
...ar, but on the third Sunday of
...eptember, the fishermen of
...aniçal bring a statue of the
...rgin by boat from their parish
...r a special service, before
...turning to Caniçal for a party.

...lantic Festival

Top 10 Festive Traditions

1 Street Decorations
When streets are turned
into tunnels of flowers, it's a
sure sign that a festival is on
the way.

2 Festive Greenery
Flower garlands hang from
poles wrapped in branches of
sweet bay.

3 Flags and Light Bulbs
Bright white bulbs light up
the night, and Madeira's flag –
a red cross on a white
background – is everywhere.

4 Firecrackers
Exploding firecrackers
mark the start of a village
festival (or a victory by one of
the local football teams).

5 Processions and Sermons
Before the fun begins, the
serious bit: a religious service
to honour the patron saint.

6 Barbecues
No village festival is
complete without delicious
beef kebabs, barbecued in an
old oil barrel.

7 Bolo de Caco
The kebabs are eaten with
spongy *bolo de caco* bread, a
soft leavened flatbread, baked
on top of a stone oven.

8 Wine
Festivals are also a
chance to sample local wines
(and cider) that are not sold
commercially.

9 Wall of Hope
At the Flower Festival,
children make a wish and pin
posies to a board in front of
the town hall.

10 Music and Dance
Brass, accordion and wind
bands, known as *filarmónicas*,
provide the music for dancing
the night away.

Left **Wickerwork demonstration** Right **Boa Vista Orchids**

Specialist Shops

1 O Relógio, Camacha
Packed to the ceiling with furniture, plant pots, baskets and lampshades, there's scarcely room to move in this Aladdin's cave of wicker. If you catch one of the wickerwork demonstrations, you'll see nimble fingers making the bending and weaving of willow canes look much easier than it really is *(see also p89)*. ✎ *Largo da Achada • Map J5 • 291 922 114*

2 Boa Vista Orchids, Funchal
Boa Vista specialize in brightly coloured *bromeliads* ("air plants"), but also grow and sell a great range of other exotic plants. ✎ *Rua Lombo da Boa Vista • Map H5 • 291 220 468*

3 Jardim Orquídea, Funchal
The Jardim Orquídea aims to convince you that growing orchids is not as difficult as you might think. Visit the laboratory and orchid garden, with its display of 50,000 plants. ✎ *Jardim Orquídea: 202 Marina Shopping Centre, Avenida Arriaga. Map Q2 • Laboratory/orchid garden: Rua Pita da Silva 37. Map H5. 291 281 941*

Orchids

4 Patricio & Gouveia, Funchal
Tour the embroidery factory to learn how traditional designs are transferred from parchment to linen, before browsing the shop for blouses, tablecloths and nightgowns with the beauty of antique lace. ✎ *Rua Visconde de Anadia 34 • Map P4 • 291 220 801*

5 Caso do Turista, Funchal
Located in the elegant 19th century former town house of the German consul, the Tourist house – which is nothing like its name – boasts a comprehensive range of Portuguese-made silver, ceramics, glassware and linen. ✎ *Rua do Conselheiro José Silvestre Ribeiro 2 • Map Q2 • 291 224 907*

6 Fado and Folk
The late-night café-music of Portuguese *fado* can become addictive. The best place to find the latest CDs by the superstars of the art – Ana Moura, Mariza, Mísia and Madredeus – is Valentim de Carvalho, the small CD shop on Funchal's main street. ✎ *Marina Shopping Centre, Avenida Arriaga 73 • Map Q2 • 291 234 920*

7 Cakes and Pastries
For delicious custard tarts *(pastéis de nata)* for immediate consumption, or *bolo de mel* (honey cake) or *amêndoa torrada* (almond sweetmeats) that will survive the journey home, try Penha d'Águia or A Lua. ✎ *Penha d'Águia: Rua das Murças 21. Map P3 • A Lua: Rua da Carreira 78. Map P2*

Leather Goods
There are fashionable leather ops aplenty in the narrow reets that lie north and south Funchal cathedral *(see pp8–9)*, ut a factory outlet called Pele eather has some of the best lue leather goods on offer, ith an extensive range of ather bags, wallets, clothing, ggage and briefcases to oose from. ◈ *Rua das Murças 26A, nchal • Map P3 • 291 223 619*

otmaker at Barros e Abreu

Barros e Abreu, Funchal
The traditional leather ankle oots made by Barros e Abreu mãos are surprisingly comfort- le, but unlike their beautiful nd timeless leather sandals, ey may look out of place back ome. Buy them from the stall the Mercado dos Lavradores *ee pp18–19)*, or see them eing made at the workshop in e Zona Velha. ◈ *Workshop: Rua do rtão de São Tiago 23 • Map Q5*

Books
Literally no more than a hole the wall, Funchal's Livraria Pátio as a good stock of books on the story, culture and wildlife of adeira, including antiquarian rities. Another Funchal bookshop lling most books on Madeira in int is the charmingly old-fash- ned Livraria Esperança. ◈ *Livraria tio: Rua da Carreira 43. Map P2. 224 0 • Livraria Esperança: Rua dos Ferreiros 9. Map N3. 291 221 116*

Top 10 Gifts to Buy

1 Embroidery
Now highly regarded by couturiers, Madeiran embroidery had unlikely beginnings; it was started by Bella Phelps in 1844 to provide work during a slump in the wine trade.

2 Tapestry
Tapestry, a close cousin of embroidery, has been produced on the island since the 1890s. Kits are available for amateur enthusiasts.

3 Wicker
Centred around Camacha, Madeira's wickerworkers create 1,200 different articles.

4 Wine and Liqueurs
As well as fortified Madeira wine, the island produces *aguardente* (translated as "rum", but actually more like brandy) and fruit liqueurs.

5 Leather
Leather bags and shoes are a Portuguese speciality.

6 Pottery
Another speciality is pottery in Moorish designs, or shaped like cabbage leaves.

7 Cakes
Festive *bolo de mel* (honey cake), once made only at Christmas, is now a year-round treat, made using cane sugar, nuts and fruit.

8 Flowers
Colourful and long-lasting blooms make a good souvenir of this garden isle.

9 Boots and Sandals
These are handmade in raw leather, to a timeless design.

10 Pompom Hats
Thick, cable-knit hats and sweaters made from raw undyed wool are worn by Madeira's farmers to keep off the chill.

Left **Adegas de São Francisco** Right **Diogos Wine Shop**

Wine Outlets

1 Adegas de São Francisco, Funchal

The St Francis Wine Lodge offers free tastings and 30-minute tours of its attics. For more in-depth information, take a special Vintage Tour *(see pp12–13)*.

2 Diogos Wine Shop, Funchal

This friendly wine shop has a surprise in the basement – a Christopher Columbus museum, put together by Mário Barbeito, founder of the Barbeito wine company in 1946. It also has a display of antique postcards and books about Madeira. ◎ *Avenida Arriaga 48 • Map P2 • 291 233 357*

3 Vinhos Barbeito, Funchal

Founded by Sr Barbeito, this wine lodge, with its distinctive chimney for the *estufa*, the "hothouse" that ages the wine, is tucked away behind Reid's Palace Hotel. The tasting room is at the rear, beyond the giant, iron-hooped barrels of American oak and satinwood. ◎ *Estrada Monumental 145 • Map H6 • 291 761 829*

Inspecting for sediment, Vinhos Barbeito

4 Artur de Barros e Sousa, Funchal

Known as ABS, this is one of Madeira's smallest producers; small, in fact, that the brothers who run it sell only to "friends – fortunately, this includes anyo who walks through the door. ◎ *dos Ferreiros 109 • Map N3 • 291 220 0*

Wine barrels, Artur de Barros e Sousa

5 D'Oliveiras, Funchal

Housed in a charming timb barn with a cobblestone floor and a carved stone door that bears the city's coat of arms ar the date AD 1619, this wine lodge offers vintages going bac to 1850, as well as younger wines, miniatures and gift boxe ◎ *Rua dos Ferreiros 107 • Map N3 • 29 220 784*

6 Loja dos Vinhos, Funchal

Conveniently located in the heart of the hotel district, and open late for last-minute gift purchases, this wine shop sells the vintages of all of Madeira's main producers, including some rare bottles that date from the 19th century. They will also take telephone orders and make hot deliveries. ◎ *Edifício Eden Mar, Loja Rua do Gorgulho • Map G6 • 291 762 8*

In 1925, the Adegas de São Francisco became the headquarters of the recently formed Madeira Wine Company.

7 Henriques & Henriques, Câmara de Lobos

Founded in 1850, the firm of Henriques & Henriques has won a string of medals and awards in recent years for its attempts to dispel the fusty image of Madeira wine and win back a younger clientele. To this end, they have introduced stylish modern labels and bottle designs, while retaining the traditional qualities of the wines themselves. 🕲 *Estrada Santa Clara 10 • Map F6 • 291 941 551*

8 Quinta do Furão, Santana

This hotel, restaurant and wine shop belonging to the Madeira Wine Company is set amid extensive vineyards near Santana, in the north of the island. Visitors can follow trails through the vineyards, and help with the harvest during late summer and early autumn (even treading grapes the old-fashioned way). 🕲 *Achada do Gramacho • Map H2 • 291 570 100*

9 Lagar d'Ajuda, Funchal

This heavily timbered shop set around an antique wine press has a comprehensive stock of ports, sherries and Portuguese regional wines, as well as Madeira from a range of island producers. 🕲 *Galerias Jardins da Ajuda, Estrada Monumental • Map G6 • 291 771 551*

10 Airport Shop, Funchal Airport

If you suddenly decide you simply cannot go home without a bottle or two of Madeira, the Madeira Wine Company has a duty-free shop at the airport, where you can buy 3-, 5-, 10- and 15-year-old wines, as well as a selection of single-grape, single-harvest vintage wines that are over 20 years old. 🕲 *Map K5*

Top 10 Madeiran Wine Terms

1 Sercial
The driest of the traditional Madeira wines – excellent as an aperitif or with soup.

2 Verdelho
A tawny, medium dry wine good for drinking with food.

3 Bual/Boal
A nutty dessert wine ideal with cheese or puddings.

4 Malmsey/Malvasia
The richest and sweetest Madeira wine, best for after-dinner drinking.

5 Dry, Medium Dry and Medium Sweet
Wines with these names are three years old, and made from *tinta negra mole* grapes. They lack the depth of real Madeira.

6 Estufagem
The process of ageing the wine in casks kept in an *estufa* (hothouse), or of heating the wine in tanks to make it age even faster. The second method yields inferior results.

7 Canteiro
The term "Canteiro" is used to distinguish quality wines and is a slow method of ageing Madeira in casks heated naturally by the sun.

8 Reserve
A blend of wines made by the two methods of *estufagem* and with an average age of five years. Made mostly with *tinta negra mole* grapes.

9 Special Reserve
A blend of wines aged in casks for about ten years. They are usually made with the noble grape varieties (1–4 above).

10 Vintage Wines
The finest Madeira, aged for a minimum of 20 years in casks and a further two years in the bottle.

For more on Madeira wine See p13

Left **Villa Cipriani** Right **Xôpana at the Choupana Hills Resort**

🔟 Restaurants

1 Les Faunes, Funchal
Reid's flagship restaurant deserves all its accolades for consistently creative cooking and polished old-world service. A special-occasion restaurant with romantic bay views. Dress code: formal. ◈ *Reid's Palace Hotel, Estrada Monumental • Map H6 • 291 71 71 71 • Closed L daily, Mon, & Jun–Sep • €€€€€*

2 Villa Cipriani, Funchal
Named after Arrigo "Harry" Cipriani and the Cipriani Hotel in Venice, this elegant restaurant is owned by Reid and has wonderful sea views and a compact menu of Italian classics. Dress code: smart casual. ◈ *Estrada Monumental • Map H6 • 291 71 71 71 • €€€€*

3 Fleur de Lys, Funchal
French classics as well as modern dishes such as grilled scallop salad with leek confit and truffle vinaigrette. Dress code: formal. ◈ *Savoy Classic Hotel, Avenida do Infante • Map H6 • 291 213 000 • Closed L daily, Sun–Mon • €€€€€*

4 Armada, Funchal
The ethnic theme of the Royal Savoy continues in the main restaurant. Try coconut prawns, five-spice beef, or duck with ginger. Dress code: smart casual. ◈ *Royal Savoy Hotel, Rua Carvalho Araújo • Map H6 • 291 213 500 • Closed L daily, Sun–Mon • €€€€*

5 Quinta da Casa Branca, Funchal
This gourmet restaurant in the 18th-century gate-house of the modern Quinta da Casa Branca hotel offers such delights as carpaccio of octopus with tomato and hazelnut-and-partridge salad with chocolate vinaigrette. Dress code: smart casual. ◈ *Rua da Casa Branca 7 • Map G6 • 291 700 770 • €€€*

6 Quinta do Monte, Monte
The furnishings may be traditional, but there's nothing old-fashioned about the menu. Try the salad of sautéed duck liver with a glass of dry Sercial wine. Dress code: smart casual. ◈ *Caminho do Monte 192 • Map H5 • 291 780 100 • €€*

7 Brasserie, Funchal
Funchal's smart set have adopted this as their canteen, enjoying such dishes as sea bass on olive potato purée. Dress code: smart casual. ◈ *Promenade do Lido • Map G6 • 291 763 325 • €€*

Brasserie

For a guide to restaurant price ranges See p71

8 Casa Velha do Palheiro, São Gonçalo

The seven-course gourmet menu at this former hunting lodge, built in 1804 by the Count of Carvalho, gathers inspiration from far and wide. Roast pigeon "Apicius" owes its origins to the ancient Roman cookery writer; gin-and-tonic sorbet is a witty reference to the country-house lifestyle; salad of fresh scallops and *foie gras* is simply delicious. Dress code: formal. ✆ Rua da Estalagem 23 • Map H6 • 291 790 350 • €€€€€

Casa Velha do Palheiro

9 Xôpana at the Choupana Hills Resort, Funchal

Designed by Didier Lefort using Asian antiques, the Xôpana is a feast for the eyes as well as the taste buds. Casual diners can enjoy a perfect beefburger, while gourmets can choose creative dishes. Dress code: smart casual. ✆ Travessa do Largo da Choupana • Map G5 • 291 206 020 • €€€

10 Boca do Cais, Funchal

This modern poolside restaurant at the Hotel Tivoli Ocean Park serves gourmet food without the high price tag that is usually attached to such dishes as fennel soup with smoked salmon, sautéed duck breast and quail, or Madeiran bouillabaisse. Dress code: smart casual. ✆ Rua Simplício dos Passos Gouveia • Map G6 • 291 702 000 • Closed L daily, Sun • €€€

Top 10 Madeiran Dishes

1 Caldo Verde
"Green soup", made with shredded kale, potatoes and onions, topped with sausage.

2 Açorda
Soup flavoured with garlic and coriander, made with bread and golden olive oil, topped off with a poached egg.

3 Espetada
Herb-flavoured barbecued beef, sometimes served on skewers that hang from a frame by your table.

4 Milho Frito
Deep-fried maize (like Italian polenta), traditionally served with *espetada*, though fries are now more common.

5 Lapas
Limpets, plucked from Madeira's rocky shores and grilled with garlic butter.

6 Bolo de Caco
Madeiran leavened flatbread, baked on top of the oven and served plain or with garlic and herb butter.

7 Espada
Scabbard fish, a succulent and (usually) boneless white fish, traditionally served grilled with fried banana.

8 Prego
Delicious Madeiran fast food – grilled steak in a bread bun (*prego special* has ham and/or cheese as well).

9 Pargo
Locally caught sea bream, delicious and nutritious simply grilled with olive oil.

10 Bacalhau
Dried salted cod – very traditional, but an acquired taste, served in many ways including with potatoes and egg, or casseroled with tomatoes and onion.

For more restaurant listings See pp71, 79, 85, 91, 99

AROUND
MADEIRA

MADEIRA'S TOP 10

Left **Funchal University courtyard** Right **Fortaleza de São Tiago**

Funchal

FOUNDED IN 1425, FUNCHAL WAS GRANTED CITY STATUS IN 1508. *As it approaches its 500th anniversary, many of its finest historical buildings are still intact, despite fire, piracy and earthquake. Named Funchal ("fennel") because of the wild fennel plants found growing in abundance by the first settlers, Madeira's capital sits on the island's southern coast in a natural amphitheatre, hemmed in by cliffs to the east and west, and steep green mountains to the north. Its streets are paved with black-and-white mosaics, and lined by blue-flowered jacaranda trees. Numerous public parks and private gardens make this a festive city of heady scents and colours, where architecture and nature are delightfully combined.*

🔟 Sights

1. Zona Velha
2. Carmo Quarter
3. Cathedral Quarter
4. Around the Town Hall
5. University Quarter
6. Around Avenida Arriaga
7. Rua da Carreira
8. São Pedro and Santa Clara
9. Hotel Zone
10. Seafront and Marina

View across Funchal to the mountains beyond

Preceding pages **Funchal's Câmara Municipal (Town Hall), set at the eastern end of the Praça do Município**

Rua Santa Maria, Zona Velha

Zona Velha
1 Funchal was the first city since Roman times to be built by Europeans outside of Europe, and the Zona Velha (Old Town) is where it began. The original settlement was protected by the Fortaleza de São Tiago, now the Museum of Contemporary Art (see p68). Today, restaurants cluster around the Capela do Corpo Santo (see p43), where fishermen and shipbuilders once had their homes. A seafront promenade and park link the Old Town to the Monte cable car station (see p52) and the covered market (see pp18–19). ◈ Map P5

Carmo Quarter
2 The Carmo Quarter lies between two of the three rivers that flow from mountain to sea through Funchal. As they pass through the city, their deep channels are overhung with purple and red bougainvillea. Linking the 17th-century Carmo Church, the Franco Museum (see p39) and IBTAM (see p68) is a warren of narrow streets, with fine buildings like the House of the Consuls (see p42). ◈ Map N4

Cathedral Quarter
3 When Christopher Columbus came to stay with his friend João Esmeraldo in 1498, the cathedral (see pp8–9) and the Alfândega (Customs House) (see p42) were still being built. Esmeraldo's home has since been transformed into the City of Sugar Museum (see p38), and the Customs House, a short step away from the sociable pavement cafés surrounding the cathedral, has become Madeira's regional parliament building. ◈ Map P3

Around the Town Hall
4 Chic clothing shops line the narrow pedestrian streets that stretch up in a grid from the cathedral to the city's one and only open square, with its fountain, its flower sellers, and its fish-scale-patterned paving. Framing the square is the graceful Baroque Câmara Municipal (Town Hall) (see p42) and the pretty, arcaded Bishop's Palace, now the Museu de Arte Sacra (Museum of Sacred Art) (see pp10–11). ◈ Map P3

Leda and the Swan, outside Town Hall

University Quarter
5 Animated saints dance and gesticulate from niches in the façade of the marvellous Igreja do Colégio (see p40), the huge and ornately decorated Jesuit church whose ancient school buildings have recently been restored to form the main campus of Madeira University (see p43). Exploring the six city blocks to the north and on either side of the campus, you will find old-fashioned bookshops, cobbled wine lodges (see p58), and some of Funchal's oldest and most ornate tower houses. ◈ Map N2

São Pedro Church

6 Around Avenida Arriaga

Wide and leafy Avenida Arriaga is lined with some of Funchal's most prestigious public buildings. They include the offices of the regional government, the imposing Bank of Portugal building *(see p43)*, the St Francis Wine Lodge *(see p58)*, the tourist office and its next-door art gallery, and the flower-filled São Francisco Gardens on the north side. On the south side is the huge São Lourenço fortress with its battlemented walls *(see p68)*,

Detail of Fortaleza de São Tiago

the Toyota showroom with its tiled exterior *(see p43)*, the theatre *(see p70)* and its chic café, and several good shopping arcades *(see p69)*. ✎ Map P2

7 Rua da Carreira

A stroll down Rua da Carreira reminds you why Funchal was once known as "Little Lisbon". The elegant buildings of this bustling street, with their green shutters and ornamental iron balconies hung with plants, are a taste of the Portuguese capital. At No. 43, the Vicentes Museum *(see p38)*, with its *belle époque* staircase, sets the theme. At the western end, a pretty *casa de prazer* (garden gazebo) sits on the corner of Rua do Quebra Costas, the street that leads to the secluded gardens of the Igreja Inglesa (English Church) *(see p42)*. ✎ Map P2

8 São Pedro and Santa Clara

The streets north of Rua da Carreira have some of Funchal's best museums. The Museu Municipal *(see p38)* in Rua Mouraria has a pretty herb garden next to it, and the church of São Pedro *(see p40)* is lined with 17th-century tiles. The steep Calçada de Santa Clara leads to the Freitas Museum *(see p38)*, Santa Clara Convent *(see pp16–17)* and the Quinta das Cruzes Museum *(see pp14–15)*. If you have energy left, keep on up to the Fortaleza do Pico ("Peak Fortress") *(see p68)* for panoramic views. ✎ Map N2

Calçada Pavements

The pavements and squares of Funchal are works of art. Blocks of dove-grey basalt and creamy limestone are laid in mosaic patterns of great intricacy and beauty, from the fish-scale pattern of the Town Hall square to the heraldic patterns and floral motifs along Avenida Arriaga. There are even complete pictures along Rua João Tavira, north of the cathedral, depicting the city's coat of arms, a wine carrier and the ship that brought Zarco *(see p15)* to Madeira.

Hotel Zone

West of the city, you can stroll through a succession of parks *(see p44)* and enjoy the varied architecture of the Art Deco mansions from the 1920s and 1930s lining the Avenida do Infante. As the road crosses the ravine of the Ribeira Seco ("Dry River") and curves past Reid's Palace, the island's most prestigious hotel *(see p112)*, mansions give way to big hotels which march along the clifftops above the city, interspersed with shopping centres and restaurants. ◈ Map Q1

Seafront and Marina

Everything in Funchal looks out to the sparkling sea and bustling harbour, where private yachts, container ships and cruise ships on transatlantic voyages call in. A stroll along Avenida do Mar allows you to soak up the sunshine, sample coffee and cakes at the onion-domed kiosks along the seafront, or wander out along the marina walls for a different view of the city. ◈ Map Q3

A Day in Old Funchal

Morning

A visit to the **cathedral** will introduce you to the two main styles of Madeiran church architecture: 16th-century Gothic and 18th-century Baroque.

Walk three blocks north to the **Sacred Art Museum**, where the island's finest works of art demonstrate how rich Madeira became when it was Europe's main source of sugar.

Enjoy Funchal's laid-back café life in one of the pavement cafés on **Praça do Município**.

Follow Rua C Pestana and Rua da Carreira westward out of the square to enjoy the lace-like balconies that decorate the upper storeys; allow half an hour to see the ceramic tile collection at the **Freitas Museum** before it closes at 12:30pm.

Afternoon

Take your pick of the restaurants along **Rua da Carreira** for a leisurely lunch, or head in the direction of the market and explore the **Zona Velha**.

Returning to Calçada de Santa Clara around 2pm, visit the shady gardens and art-filled rooms of the **Quinta das Cruzes**; then take a guided tour of Santa Clara Convent.

Wind down after a day of culture by taking the 4:30pm tour of the St Francis Wine Lodge – the oldest on Madeira.

Finish the day with a stroll along Avenida do Mar, or enjoy the harbour view from Santa Catarina Park.

Funchal Marina

Left **Cemitério Britânico**

🔟 Best of the Rest

1 Museu de Arte Contemporânea

The 17th-century Fortaleza de São Tiago makes a superb setting for late 20th-century works of art. ◎ *Rua do Portão de São Tiago • Map Q6 • 291 213 340 • 10am– 12:30pm, 2–5:30pm Mon–Sat • Adm charge*

2 Museu de Electricidade "Casa da Luz"

This former power station shows what heroic efforts were needed to bring electricity to the island. ◎ *Rua da Casa da Luz 2 • Map P4 • 291 211 480 • 10am–12:30pm, 2–6pm Tue–Sat • Adm charge*

3 Núcleo Museológico do Bordado

The history of embroidery, tapestry and handicrafts on Madeira, with an introduction to the island's colourful costumes. Formerly known as IBTAM. ◎ *Rua do Visconde do Anadia 44 • Map N4 • 291 223 141 • 10am– 12:30pm, 2–5:30pm Mon–Fri • Adm charge*

4 Museu do Instituto do Vinho da Madeira

Displays on wine production in the house of the Napoleonic-era British consul Henry Veitch. ◎ *Rua 5 de Outubro 78 • Map N3 • 291 204 600 • 9am–6pm Mon–Fri • Free*

5 Palácio de São Lourenço

The historic fortress has displays on the pirate Bertrand de Montluc *(see p31).* ◎ *Avenida Zarco • Map P3 • 9:30am–noon, 2–5:30pm Tue–Sat (closed Sat pm) • Free*

6 Cemitério Britânico

Protestants of all nations a buried in this garden-like cemeto whose ancient headstones tel many a poignant story. ◎ *Rua da Carreira 331 • Map P1 • 9:30am–12:30p, 2–5pm Mon–Fri (ring bell at gate) • Fre*

7 Fortaleza do Pico

The stiff uphill walk to the 17th-century Peak Fortress is r warded by sweeping views an one-room museum on the histo of Funchal's defences. ◎ *Rua do Forte • Map N1 • 9am–6pm Mon–Sat • F*

8 Lido Promenade

A new seafront promenade follows the clifftops west of the city from the Lido to Praia Formosa, with landscaped gardens and ever-changing views. ◎ *Rua Gorgulho • Map G6*

9 Museu do Brinquedo (Toy Museum)

From 19th-century china dolls t 1980s plastic Barbies, over 100 years of toy history, with a hug collection of miniature cars. The is a restaurant on the ground floor. ◎ *Rua da Levada dos Barreiros 4 • Map G6 • 919 922 722 • 2–6pm Mon, 10am–6pm Tue–Sat • Adm charge*

10 Museu Barbeito Cristóvão Colombo

One man's passion for Columb led to this collection of historic books, engravings and portraits ◎ *Avenida Arriaga 48 • Map P2 • 291 2 357 • 9:30am–1pm, 3–6pm Mon–Sat (closed Sat pm) • Adm charge*

Cabbage leaf plate, Casa do Turista *Right* Embroidery at Bazar Oliveiras

Places to Shop

Mercado dos Lavradores
Make it a daily habit while in [Fun]chal to visit the market and [sho]p for picnic ingredients or [so]uvenirs, or simply savour the [col]ourful bustle *(see pp18–19)*.

Madeira Shopping
Madeira Shopping provides [ret]ail therapy for shopaholics: top [Eu]ropean brands, and over 100 [sto]res in one mall. Follow signs [fro]m the São Martinho exit of [th]e Via Rapida, or take the free [sh]uttle bus (weekdays only) from [th]e hotel zone. ✪ *Caminho de Santa [Qui]téria 45, Santo António• Map G5*

Casa do Turista
All the elegance of a bygone [er]a: Madeiran and mainland [Por]tuguese textiles, ceramics, [sil]ver and glassware displayed in [a] stately town house. ✪ *Rua do [Con]selheiro José Silvestre Ribeiro 2 [(bel]ow the Teatro Municipal) • Map Q2*

Galerias São Lourenço
At Funchal's most upmarket [sho]pping mall you will find [ev]erything from sunglasses and [chi]ldren's clothes to elegant [kit]chen- and tableware. ✪ *Avenida [Arri]aga 41 • Map P2*

Arcadas de São Francisco
The cobbled yard where [th]e barrels were once made [for] the São Francisco Wine [Lo]dge is now a mall selling top-[br]and fashions, ethnic-inspired [fur]nishings and jewellery. ✪ *Rua [de] São Francisco 20 • Map P2*

Marina Shopping Centre
Three floors packed with every kind of shop, from surf clothing to books, and from chic shoes and bags to antique postcards. ✪ *Avenida Arriaga 75 • Map Q2*

Rua das Murças
Come to this narrow city-centre street for keenly priced shops like Bazar Oliveiras (No. 6), selling leather, embroidery, tapestry, and all kinds of Madeiran souvenirs. Most shops open 10am–8pm daily. ✪ *Map P3*

Antiques Quarter
Shops selling contemporary art or old maps and engravings, chests, chandeliers, mirrors and Chinese spice jars, furniture and clocks. ✪ *Rua da Mouraria and Rua de São Pedro • Map P2, N2*

Bazar do Povo
Opposite the cathedral, Funchal's oldest department store has been well maintained over the years and lives up to its name ("People's Bazaar") by stocking everything from DVDs to religious statues. ✪ *Largo do Chafariz/Rua do Aljube • Map P3*

Rua Dr. Fernão Ornelas
Funchal's main shopping street is a wonderful mix of chic boutiques sitting cheek-by-jowl with grocers selling coffee and pungent salt cod. Most shops close on Saturday afternoon and Sunday. ✪ *Map P4*

Left **Casino da Madeira** Right **Teatro Municipal**

Nights Out

1 The Evening Stroll
Do as Madeirans do and come out for the evening *passeio* along the seafront, grazing on sweet pastries from the stalls along Avenida do Mar. ◈ *Map Q3*

2 Teatro Municipal
The resplendent theatre (built 1888) hosts music recitals, contemporary dance, drama (usually in Portuguese) and art-house movies. Look for billboards outside the theatre. ◈ *Avenida Arriaga • Map P2 • 291 220 416*

3 Café do Teatro
The romantic night-time haunt of Funchal's smart set, this small but sophisticated café, in a palm-shaded courtyard beside the theatre, offers cocktails, chat and occasional DJs. ◈ *Avenida Arriaga 40 • Map P2 • 291 226 371*

4 Casino da Madeira
As well as playing slot machines, roulette and blackjack, you can also come here for live music in the Copacabana Bar, or the dinner shows on Wednesday, Friday, Saturday and Sunday. ◈ *Avenida do Infante (in the grounds of the Pestana Casino Park Hotel) • Map H6 • 291 209 180*

5 Chameleon Music Bar
Funchal's night owls dance their cares away at the friendliest disco-bar in town, with resident DJ and live band on Wednesdays. ◈ *Rua Carvalho Araújo • Map H6 • 291 228 038*

6 Discoteca Vespas
Three resident DJs, an international mix of pop and ro[ck], top-quality sound, spectacular laser, and youthful atmosphere[.] ◈ *Avenida Sá Carneiro 7 (opposite th[e] container port) • Map Q2 • 291 234 8[*

7 O'Farol
Golden oldies and popular chart hits have made "The Lighthouse" a favourite disco f[or] those who are too old for Vespa[s] but still like to dance the night away. ◈ *Pestana Carlton Hotel, Larg[o] António Nobre • Map H6 • 291 239 5[*

8 Marcelino Pão e Vinho
One voice, two guitars, perhaps an accordion – Portuga[l's] *fado* music (meaning "fate") is poetic and bittersweet. This lat[e] night wine bar is Funchal's mos[t] authentic venue. ◈ *Travessa da To[rre] 22A • Map P5 • 291 220 216*

9 Folk Music and Dance
Madeira's *charamba* was sung to ease the daily grind. Roving bands of musicians and dancers visit the Marina Terrac[e] on Avenida do Mar most evenin[g] – alternatively, you can book a show at the Cliff Bay Resort Hotel. ◈ *Cliff Bay: Estrada Monumen[tal] 147 • Map G6 • 291 707 707*

10 Classical Concerts
Funchal's Mandoline Orch-estra, the Orquestra Clássica d[e] Madeira, and the Brass Ensem[ble] perform several times a month[.] See posters on Avenida Arriaga[.]

For a three course	
meal for one with half	€ under €15
a bottle of wine (or	€€ €15–€25
equivalent meal), taxes	€€€ €25–€40
and extra charges.	€€€€ €40–€60
	€€€€€ over €60

twell

10 Places to Eat

1 Zarco's
It's worth the short taxi ride to sit on a terrace with a classic westerly view of Funchal Harbour while dining on classic Madeiran *espetadas* of beef, chicken and fish from the open grill. ✎ *Estrada Monde Carvalhal 136A, São Gonçalo • Map J6 • 291 795 599 • €€*

2 Arsénio's
Listen to live *fado* (traditional Portuguese café music) every night at 8pm while dining on succulent kebabs in the Zona Velha (Old Town). ✎ *Rua da Santa Maria 169 • Map P5 • 291 224 007 • €€€*

3 Eatwell
This small restaurant belongs to a catering school which means that dishes and service are of a standard that would usually cost more. Well presented starters include salads and duck breasts grilled on a eucalyptus wood fire. ✎ *Rua Dr. Pita 23a • Map G6 • 291 764 020 • Closed during catering events) • €€€*

4 Arco Velho
Among the many pavement cafés of the Zona Velha (Old Town), the Arco Velho stands out for value. Try a plate of grilled sardines and salad, with a glass of local white wine. ✎ *Rua Dom Carlos I 42 • Map P5 • 291 225 683 • €*

5 Marina Terrace
One of a cluster of open-air seafood restaurants set around the marina. ✎ *Cais da Cidade Marina • Funchal • Map Q3 • 291 230 547 • €€€*

6 É pra Picanha
Brazilian specialities such as *picanha* (grilled rump of beef) and *feijoada* (black-bean stew). Some fish and seafood; local scabbard fish is served with a passion fruit sauce. ✎ *Edifício Infante Dom Henrique 206, Avenida do Infante • Map H6 • 291 282 257 • Closed Sat L, Sun • €€*

7 Taj Mahal
Try tandoori king prawn, fish tikka massala and *gulfi* ice cream at this stylish Indian restaurant set in a glass conservatory behind the Savoy. ✎ *Rua Imperatriz Dona Amélia 119 • Map H6 • 291 228 038 • €€*

8 Doca do Cavacas
This rustic beachside bar is renowned for freshly caught fish served to the sound of crashing waves. ✎ *Rua Ponta da Cruz (western end of Estrada Monumental) • Map G6 • 291 762 057 • €€*

9 O Barqueiro
Arguably the best and most varied fish restaurant on Madeira. If you're spoilt for choice, try the "tasting menu", but avoid the over-priced lobster. ✎ *Rua Ponta da Cruz (western end of Estrada Monumental) • Map G6 • 291 765 226 • €€€*

10 Brasserie
Its red walls, black furniture and white napery spell sophis-tication. The cooking is new-wave Italian. There's a choice of vege-tarian dishes. ✎ *Promenade do Lido (Hotel Zone, below Hotel Tivoli) • Map G6 • 291 763 325 • Closed Mon, Tue L • €€€*

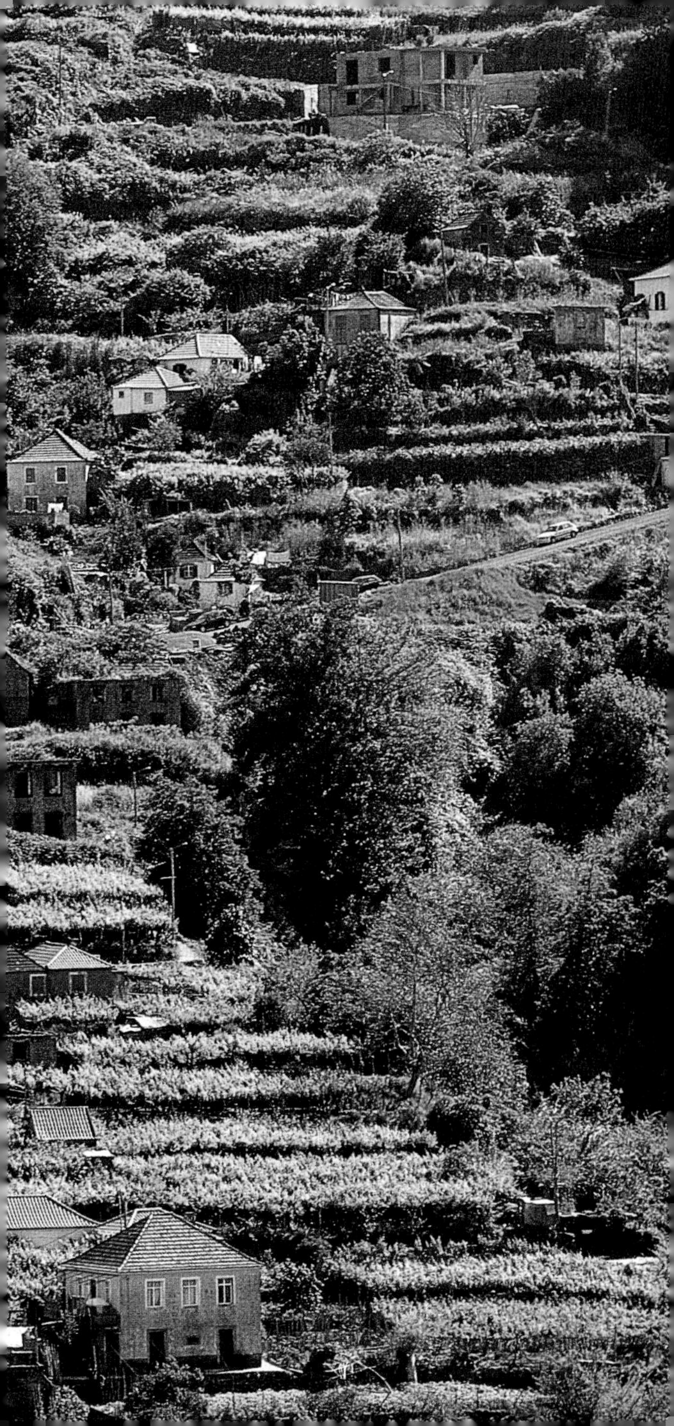

Quinta do Palheiro Ferreiro (Blandy's Gardens)

Central Madeira

CENTRAL MADEIRA CONSISTS ALMOST ENTIRELY *of high volcanic peak and deep ravines. To experience this scenic grandeur to the full you really do have to walk, but thanks to some well-placed miradouros (scenic viewing points), you can come away with some memorable photographs c gain a sense of the immense visual appeal of the central mountain range*

even when travelling by road. Between the north and the south there are great contrasts. Soaked in sunshine, the southern slopes are densely populated, with red-tiled farmhouses lost in a sea of vines and bananas. The northern slopes are densely wooded; along the coastal strip, tiny terraces cling to the steep valley sides making a colourful patchwork of many different hues of green.

Câmara de Lobos

Sights

1. Monte
2. Quinta do Palheiro Ferreiro
3. Jardim Botânico
4. Câmara de Lobos
5. Cabo Girão
6. Curral das Freiras
7. Pico do Arieiro
8. Ribeiro Frio
9. Santana
10. Pico Ruivo

Preceding pages **Step-like terraces cut into a hillside near São Vicente, Western Madeira**

nte cable car

Câmara de Lobos

The *lobos* ("wolves") in the name of this pretty village refer to the monk seals that once basked on the pebbly beach *(see p46)*. This is now used as an open-air boatyard, where traditional craft are repaired or given a fresh coat of blue, red and yellow paint, laid on in bold stripes. Down among the noisy bars is the Fishermen's Chapel, where villagers give thanks for the safe return of their men after a long night at sea, fishing for *espada* (scabbard fish), most of which ends up on the tables of Madeira's many restaurants.
⊗ *Map F6 • All Rodoeste buses call here*

Monte

Take the cable car from nchal's Zona Velha up to onte, and you will sail 600 m 968 ft) up the southern face of adeira to a place that seems re garden than village, shaded veteran trees and watered by tural springs *(see pp26–7)*.

Quinta do Palheiro Ferreiro

anks to a period spent in exile England during the early 19th ntury, the first owner of this tate, the Count of Carvalhal, veloped a love of meadows, ods and streams, and laid e foundations for today's richly ried garden *(see pp24–5)*.

Jardim Botânico

Come here to satisfy ur curiosity about the mes and origins of all e flowering trees, palms, cculents and scented mbers that grow every- ere in Madeira – in nt gardens, in public rks and along country ads *(see pp20–21)*.

Cabo Girão

Madeira's highest sea cliff, 580m (1,903 ft) above the ocean, also claims to be the second highest in the world, but opinions differ over the location of the highest: some say Norway, others the Orkneys or Ireland. From the viewing point perched on the summit, you gaze down to a *fajã*, a rock platform created when part of the cliff face fell into the sea millennia ago. Local farmers cultivate crops here in neat terraces. If you want a closer look, you can take the cable car *(teleférico)* from Caldeira Rancho, on the western side of Câmara de Lobos, down to the base of the cliff. ⊗ *Map E5 • No bus*

Jardim Botânico (Botanical Gardens)

View of Curral das Freiras

6 Curral das Freiras

A new road-tunnel now links the valley village of Curral das Freiras with the wider world, but for breathtaking views, travel along the old road via Eira do Serrado. By taking this route, you will also gain a sense of just how isolated this community once was (see pp30–31).

7 Pico do Arieiro

In the colourful landscape of Madeira's third highest peak you can read the story of the volcanic forces that created the island, and the elemental battles between wind, rock and rain that eroded it into jagged peaks and plunging ravines (see pp32–3).

A-framed Houses

The colourful A-framed houses of the Santana district were probably introduced by early settlers from the farming districts of central Portugal. Today they are used as houses, or as cattle byres. On an island of precipitous slopes, cattle can easily fall if left to graze freely, so they are kept in the cool shade of the thatched *palheiros*, to which their owners carry stacks of freshly cut grass and foliage at intervals during the day.

8 Ribeiro Frio

The "Cold River" of this valley clearing tumbles down the mountainside to bring clear water to a trout farm set in a pretty garden planted with Madeira's native flowers. Some of the trout inevitably end up on the menu of the Restaurante Ribeiro Frio opposite, a good place to begin or end a short walk along the dry *levada* to Balcões (see p51). A longer walk to Portela starts just below the restaurant; you need a map and guidebook to do the whole route, but you can enjoy splendid views of the dense green forest by sampling the first stretch. ◎ Map H4 • São Roque de Faial bus 132

9 Santana

Santana has Madeira's best examples of the traditional

A-framed houses, Santana

The weather on Pico do Arieiro is often clearest in the first part the morning and in the evening, so plan your walk accordingly.

nber-and-thatch dwellings
own as *palheiros*. These
ghtly-painted triangular houses
e comfortable but compact,
d many now have modern
tensions to accommodate the
chens and bathrooms that the
ginals lacked. You can visit and
ke photographs of a row of
urist-board houses next to the
urch, but wander the lanes of
e village and you will see
enty more, with immaculate
rdens. ◈ *Map H2 • São Roque de
al bus 103 or SAM buses 53 and 78*

w from Pico Ruivo

Pico Ruivo
Madeira's highest peak is
iched from the road next to
petrol station on the eastern
e of Santana. This leads to the
park at Achada do Teixeira,
m where a well-paved path
mbs to the summit (1,862 m,
09 ft). To the south, the views
k over the high peaks and
ged ridges of an arid volcanic
dscape; to the north, clouds
ng around the lush, forested
pes. Back at the car park, look
the eroded rocks called
mem em Pé ("Standing Man")
hollow behind the rest
use. ◈ *Map G3 • No bus*

A Day in Central Madeira

Morning

🕙 Starting in **Monte** by 10am
at the latest, your first stop
is the summit of **Pico do
Arieiro**. (If it's too cloudy,
do the trip in reverse; the
weather may clear later on.)

Afterward, descend to
Ribeiro Frio to visit the
trout farm and enjoy the
native Madeiran flowers in
the surrounding gardens.

Walk downhill past the
shop, and take the *levada*
path signposted left to
Balcões. A 20-minute
stroll through woodland
brings you to a cutting in
the rock with wonderful
views over the island's
central peaks and valleys.

For lunch, try **Restaurante
Ribeiro Frio** *(see p79)*, or
continue on to **Santana**. If
you prefer to bring your
own food, there are picnic
tables around Ribeiro Frio.

Afternoon

If you're not already in
Santana, make your way
there; the main attractions
are the traditional triangular
houses. Next, follow signs
to the Rocha do Navio
Teleférico, and you will
find a cable car and footpath to **Santana's beach**.

Now head west into **Faial**.
Two "balconies" along the
way give you memorable
views of **Penha de Águia**
("Eagle Rock"). In Faial
itself, there are numerous
signposted walks.

If you're staying in Funchal,
the fastest route back is to
follow signs to Machico
through a long tunnel that
links up at the southern
end with the airport road
back to the city.

Old sugar mill, Porto da Cruz

🔟 Best of the Rest

1 Terreiro da Luta
Pious Madeirans believe that the Virgin appeared to a young shepherd girl on this spot and gave her the statue now in Monte church. The present memorial was erected after German U-boats attacked ships in Funchal Harbour in 1916; the Virgin's help was sought and the bombardment stopped. ◈ Map H5

2 Queimadas
From western Santana, a road signposted to "Queimadas" gives way to a track leading to a house with gardens, ponds and picnic tables deep in the green-wooded heart of the UNESCO World Natural Heritage forest. ◈ Map H3

3 Caldeirão Verde
From Queimadas, take a scenic *levada* walk to the "Green Cauldron", a waterfall cascading down a rock hollow. Sturdy foot-wear, torches (flashlights) and waterproofs essential. ◈ Map G3

4 Ponta Delgada
At Ponta Delgada's church, see the miraculous statue, found floating at sea in the 16th century. When the church burned down in 1908, it was found charred but intact in the embers. ◈ Map F2

5 Boaventura
Boaventura makes a great base for exploring the orchards watered by the Levada de Cima. Make sure to take a good walking guide *(see p50)*. ◈ Map G2

6 São Jorge
São Jorge has a Baroque church from 1761. A 19th-centu[ry] lighthouse sits on Ponta de Sã[o] Jorge, with views of the coast A side road east of the village leads to a small, sheltered bea[ch] *(see p46)*. ◈ Map H2

7 Faial
The Fortím do Faial is a to[wn] town fort built in the 18th centu[ry] to fend off pirates. South of the village are views of Penha de Águia and the newly formed r[ock] platform *(fajã)* where part of th[e] cliff fell into the sea. ◈ Map J3

8 Penha de Águia
"Eagle Rock" rises 590 m (180 ft) from the sea, casting its shadow over neighbouring villages. Young Madeirans regar[d] the climb from Penha de Águia de Baixo to the top as a test of strength and endurance. ◈ Map [J3]

9 São Roque de Faial
Several valleys meet at Sã[o] Roque, so walkers can start at the church and choose one of the paths that go west up the Ribeiro Frio ("Cold River") or e[ast] up the Tem-te Não Caias (litera[lly] "Hold on; don't fall"). ◈ Map J3

10 Porto da Cruz
The Old Town is a maze of cobbled alleys and old wine warehouses. A sugar mill stan[ds] by the harbour, where visitors can buy the aged, locally distil[led] spirit *aguardente*. ◈ Map J3

Price Categories

For a three course meal for one with half a bottle of wine (or equivalent meal), taxes and extra charges.

€	under €15
€€	€15–€25
€€€	€25–€40
€€€€	€40–€60
€€€€€	over €60

...a de Abrigo de Poiso

🔟 Places to Eat

1 Jasmin Tea House, São Gonçalo

...is is a popular spot for walkers ...ploring the Levada dos Tornos (...ee p51). The English owners ...rve home-made soups, tea ...th scones, and delicious ...kes. 🛇 *Caminho dos Pretos 40* ...*Map H6* • *291 792 796* • *€*

2 Hortensia Gardens Tea House, São Gonçalo

...rther west from the Levada ...s Tornos, the Hortensia serves ...up and cake to hungry walkers. ...*Caminho dos Pretos 89* • *Map H6* ...*91 792 179* • *€*

3 Churrascaria O Lagar, Câmara de Lobos

...is big, pink palace serves ...rfectly tender garlic-flavoured ...icken and skewers of beef, with ...arm rounds of cake-like *bolo de* ...*co* bread, liberally soaked in ...rlic butter. 🛇 *Estrada do João G* ...*rco 478* • *Map F6* • *291 941 865* • *€€*

4 Lobos Mar, Câmara de Lobos

...hoose from limpets or winkles, ...ast chicken or grilled fish; or try ...e tripe *(dobrada)* or the beef and ...an stew *(feijoada)*. 🛇 *Rua São João Deus 8* • *Map F6* • *291 942 379* • *€*

5 As Vides, Estreito de Câmara de Lobos

...u can smell the wood-smoke ...s you near this 1950s log cabin ...rving grilled meats from an ...en fire. 🛇 *Rua da Achada 17, Sítio* ...*Igreja* • *Map F6* • *291 945 322* • *€€*

6 Nun's Valley, Curral das Freiras

Delicious dishes based on the local chestnut crop: roasted and salted; with vegetables in a tasty soup; in a delicious cake; and as a liqueur. 🛇 *Casas Próximas* • *Map F4* • *291 712 177* • *€€*

7 Eira do Serrado

Poised 500 m (1640 ft) above Curral das Freiras, you could come here just for the fine view, but the food is also first class, with a good choice of grilled meats and fish. 🛇 *Map G4* • *291 710 060* • *€€€*

8 Casa de Abrigo de Poiso, Poiso Pass

It's often cooler and wetter here than elsewhere in Madeira, hence the big open fire at this mountain-pass timber lodge. The glowing embers make delicious barbecued Madeiran kebabs. 🛇 *Map E2* • *291 782 269* • *€€*

9 Restaurante Ribeiro Frio

Located opposite a spring-fed trout farm, this woodland lodge serves both smoked and grilled trout, trout pâté and home-made puddings. Wash it down with a glass of local cider. 🛇 *Map H4* • *291 575 898* • *€€*

🔟 Escola Profissional de Hotelaria, São Martinho

Eat where Madeira's chefs and waiters receive their training; the hotel school offers lunch, tea and dinner, crisply served. 🛇 *Travessa dos Piornais* • *Map G6* • *291 700 386* • *€€€*

Left **Paúl da Serra** Right **Seixal**

Western Madeira

THE VALLEY ROAD LINKING RIBEIRA BRAVA AND SÃO VICENTE *via the Encumeada Pass* forms the boundary between the high peaks of central Madeira and the flat, treeless moorland of the Paúl da Serra plateau to the west. Scores of ridges and ravines run down the plateau escarpment, like pleats in a skirt. Those to the north plunge almost sheer to the sea, with waterfalls that cascade for hundreds of feet. Farming villages cling to the gentler slopes to the south and west, where new roads are beginning to open up beautiful parts of the island which few visitors have yet explored.

Porto Moniz

🔟 Sights

1 Ribeira Brava
2 Boca da Encumeada
3 São Vicente
4 Seixal
5 Porto Moniz
6 Ponta do Pargo
7 Jardim do Mar
8 Calheta
9 Paúl da Serra
🔟 Rabaçal

Ribeira Brava

1 Ribeira Brava (literally, "Wild River") is one of the island's oldest towns, well established as a centre of sugar production by the 1440s. The large parish church has sculpture dating from the 1480s. At the other end of the village is the Museu Etnográfico da Madeira *(see p39)*, with a small shop selling Madeiran crafts. ◈ *Map D5 • Rodoeste buses 4, 7, 80, 107, 115, 139 and 142*

Boca da Encumeada

2 The Encumeada Pass is a saddle of rock forming the watershed between the north and south of the island. Clouds from the north often spill over the lip of the mountains, like dry ice pouring from a flask. Wherever you look, there are majestic peaks, from Pico Grande in the east to cone-shaped Crista de Galo in the west. Just south of the pass is the Levada do Norte (signposted "Folhadel"), which offers a lovely 15-minute walk to the point where it enters a tunnel. *Map E3 • Rodoeste buses 6 and 139*

São Vicente

3 This pretty village on the northern side of the Encumeada Pass demands to be captured in paint; deep-green shutters, doors and balconies, with stone lintels and frames of ox-blood red, are set in white-walled houses along the grey basalt streets. ◈ *Map E2 • Rodoeste buses 6 and 139*

Boca da Encumeada – the view south

São Vicente

Seixal

4 Most of the coastal road now runs through tunnels, but Seixal is one of the few places where you can still get a sense of the north coast's visual splendour. Tall cliffs stretching into the distance are pounded by powerful waves that swell and break at their feet. Vineyards cling to the rock on almost vertical terraces. Waterfalls plunge from the wooded heights on either side of the village. ◈ *Map D2 • Rodoeste buses 80 and 139*

Porto Moniz

5 Porto Moniz, the most northwesterly conurbation on the island, combines a bustling agricultural town set high up around its church, with a lower town devoted to food and bathing. Natural rock pools have been turned into a bathing complex offering a safe environment in which to enjoy the exhilarating experience of being showered by spray from waves breaking on the offshore rocks. The newly landscaped seafront is lined with restaurants selling some of the island's best seafood. ◈ *Map B1 • Rodoeste buses 80 and 139*

Lighthouse, Ponta do Pargo

6 Ponta do Pargo

Madeira's westernmost point, Ponta do Pargo is the best place on the island to watch the setting sun or to gaze down at the waves breaking along the tall cliffs of the island's southern and western coasts. The lighthouse on the headland (built in 1896) has a small exhibition of maps and photographs charting the history of lighthouses on every island in the Madeiran archipelago. The ceiling of the parish church is covered with colourful paintings of sunsets, terraced hills, and the scenic spots of the western part of the island, all painted in the 1990s by a Belgian artist who has settled in the village. ◐ Map A2 • Rodoeste buses 107 and 142

7 Jardim do Mar

This pretty village (literally, "Garden of the Sea") sits at the meeting-point of several ancient cobbled foot-paths, which climb up the cliffs to either side. In the village itself, a maze of alleys winds down to a pebble beach where surfing competitions are held during the winter months. A new seafront road and a large sea-wall were completed in 2004; opinions vary as to how this has affected the quality of the surfing here. ◐ Map B4 • Rodoeste bus 142

8 Calheta

Calheta's fine parish church, a scaled-down version of Funchal cathedral (see pp8–9), stands on a terrace halfway up the hill leading west out of the village. It has a precious 16th-century ebony-and-silver tabernacle, and a richly decorated knotwork ceiling above the high altar. Next door to the church is the Engenho da Calheta, one of Madeira's two surviving sugar mills; the other is in Porto da Cruz (see p78). As well as producing mel (honey), used in making the island's unique bolo de mel (honey cake), the mill also makes aguardente (rum) from distilled cane syrup. ◐ Map B4 • Rodoeste bus 142 • Calheta Church: open 10am–1pm, 4–6pm daily • Engenho da Calheta: 291 822 264. Open 9am–7pm Mon–Fri, 10am–7pm Sat–Sun

9 Paúl da Serra

The undulating plateau of Paúl da Serra ("Mountain Marsh") is the gathering point for the waters that feed many of the island's rivers and levadas. It serves as a sponge for the abundant rains which fall when clouds reach the island, rise, then cool. Free-range horned

Sugar Revival

The sugar mills at Calheta and Porto da Cruz date from the sugar renaissance of the 19th century, when the demand for high-quality sugar rose dramatically, thanks to the popularity of sweetmeats in genteel European households. The nuns of Santa Clara (see p16) were especially renowned for their preserves, marzipan sweets, crystallized figs and other delights.

ttle graze the lush grass.
eople from the surrounding
llages come here in summer
o pick wild bilberries and black-
erries, which they turn into
elicious conserves. Many of
nem also depend on the
lateau's forest of wind turbines
o supply them with electricity.
Map D3 • Rodoeste bus 139

Rabaçal

Washed by centuries of
ain running from the flat,
nonotonous surface of the Paúl
a Serra, Rabaçal is a magical
reen cleft in the moorland. A
risk 2-km (1-mile) walk down a
vinding tarmac path takes you
nrough stands of heather and
room to a forest house with
cnic tables. Rabaçal marks the
tart of two popular walks (both
gnposted). One follows the
evada do Risco to the Risco
Vaterfall (30 minutes there and
ack); the other follows the next
rrace down to 25 Fontes
'25 Springs"), a cauldron-like
ool fed by numerous cascades
hour 40 minutes there and
ack). *Map C3 • Rodoeste bus 139*

sco Falls, Rabaçal

A Day in Western Madeira

Morning

First stop on this long but
rewarding trip is **Ribeira
Brava**, 25 minutes from
Funchal by the south coast
highway. If you arrive
before the **Ethnography
Museum** opens *(see p39)*,
enjoy a coffee on the seafront or call in at the church.

Driving north, follow signs
to **Serra de Água**. For
spectacular mountain
views, avoid the new tunnel
route to São Vicente.

Descending to **São
Vicente**, spare some time
for a short but fascinating
tour of the lava caves on
the east bank of the river.

Take the old corniche road
("Antiga 101") to **Porto
Moniz**. The rock pools of
the lower town are a great
place to relieve tension
after the drive. Follow a
dip with lunch in any of
the nearby fish restaurants.

Afternoon

Drive back along the road
to **São Vicente** for 2 km
(1 mile), then turn right to
Ribeira da Janela. Beyond
the village, the road climbs
through a wild landscape
of native Madeiran forest.

Continue as far as the **Paúl
da Serra** plateau. Taking
the next two right turns,
make for the car park above
Rabaçal. Allow two hours
to explore this woodland
world of birdsong, running
water, fern-hung rocks and
ancient tree heaths.

To return to Funchal, take
the Encumeada Pass, turn
left to Vargem, then left
again to join the long tunnel
that joins the south coast
highway at Ribeira Brava.

Left **Ribeira da Janela** Right **Ponta do Sol**

Best of the Rest

1 Ribeira da Janela
This wild, uninhabited valley 18 km (11 miles) long, joins the sea beside a rocky islet with a window-like hole (hence the name, "Window Valley"). The road descends through a misty world of ancient trees kept moist by the condensation of clouds. ◈ *Map C1*

2 Fanal
This forest house halfway up the Ribeira de Janela is the starting point for walks that lead through an alpine landscape of herb-rich meadows, filled with ancient laurel trees. ◈ *Map C2*

3 Ponta do Sol
The American novelist John dos Passos (1896–1970) visited this sun-trap village in 1960 to see his grandparents' house – now being turned into a cultural centre. ◈ *Map D5*

4 Lombada
On a ridge above Ponta do Sol is one of Madeira's oldest houses – the 15th-century mansion of Columbus's friend João Esmeraldo (*see p65*). The watermill opposite is fed by one of the island's oldest *levadas*. A pretty church of 1722 is lined with tile pictures of the Virtues. ◈ *Map D5*

5 Arco da Calheta
Another early church survives at the heart of this sprawling village – the mid-15th-century Capela do Loreto, founded by the wife of Zarco's grandson. ◈ *Map C4*

6 Lombo dos Reis
The "Ridge of the Kings" is named after the tiny, rustic Cape dos Reis Magos ("Chapel of the Three Kings"), which has a rare early 16th-century Flemish altar carving of the Nativity. ◈ *Map B4*

7 Lugar de Baixo
Above the tiny freshwater lagoon at Lugar de Baixo is a visitor centre with pictures of the wild birds that frequent this rocky shore, though you are more likely to see domesticated ducks and moorhens. ◈ *Map D5*

8 Prazeres
The priest at Prazeres has established a small children's farm opposite the church, but the main attraction is the flower-lined path along the Levada Nov ("New Levada"), which can be followed east or west. ◈ *Map B3*

9 Paúl do Mar
The best approach to this fishing (and surfing) village is down the twisting road from Fa de Orvela. On the way, look out for a glimpse of the stunning Galinas Gorge. ◈ *Map A3*

10 Cristo Rei
This statue of Christ (on the ER209 road to Paúl da Serra) is reminiscent of the famous one in Rio de Janeiro. It is also the starting point for easy *levada* walks – west to the Paúl da Serra east to the waterfalls at Cascalho ◈ *Map D4*

Cachalote, Porto Moniz

Price Categories		
For a three course	€	under €15
meal for one with half	€€	€15–€25
a bottle of wine (or	€€€	€25–€40
equivalent meal), taxes	€€€€	€40–€60
and extra charges.	€€€€€	over €60

10 Places to Eat

1 Pousada dos Vinháticos, Serra de Água

The food is perfectly good but the views steal the limelight. Picture windows look out onto Madeira's most Wagnerian mountain landscapes, lit by the setting sun. *Map E4 • 291 952 344 • €€€*

2 O Virgílio, São Vicente

"Virgil's" stands out from the other seafront fish restaurants in São Vicente for its eccentric decor, authentic Madeiran atmosphere and perfect sardines. *Map E2 • 291 842 467 • €€*

3 O Cachalote, Porto Moniz

Long regarded as the best seafood restaurant in Porto Moniz, Cachalote now has competition from several new restaurants in this popular resort. ◈ *Praia do Porto Moniz • Map B1 • 291 853 180 • €€*

4 Orca, Porto Moniz

The circular dining room with its big windows maximizes the views over the rock pools of Porto Moniz, adding savour to a menu that features *caldeirada* (fish casserole), red bream and sea bass. ◈ *Praia do Porto Moniz • Map B1 • 291 850 000 • €€*

5 Casa de Chá "O Fío", Ponta do Pargo

A teahouse isn't what you'd expect to find on a clifftop, but many make the pilgrimage for hearty home-made soups, and dishes of cod with sweet peppers. *Map A2 • €€*

6 Jardim Atlântico, Prazeres

The best bet for vegetarians looking for an escape from an endless diet of omelettes, the restaurant at the Jardim Atlântico Hotel sources its produce from local market gardens. ◈ *Lombo da Rocha • Map B3 • 291 820 220 • €€€*

7 Jungle Rain, Sítio do Ovil

This themed restaurant full of (plastic) tree trunks and tropical creepers is in the middle of the bleak Paúl do Mar plateau. The menu of pasta and spaghetti bolognese makes it a firm family favourite. ◈ *Estalagem Pico da Urze • Map C3 • 291 820 150 • €€*

8 Tarmar, Jardim do Mar

This simple, unpretentious restaurant on the eastern side of the village is one of the best in the area for fish and seafood. There's a small bougainvillea-shaded terrace. ◈ *Map B4 • 291 823 207 • €€*

9 Santo António, nr Ribeira Brava

With its smart roof shaped like a wave, this swish new glass-and-wood restaurant is a great choice for seafood. ◈ *Lugar de Baixo • Map D5 • 291 972 868 • €€€*

10 O Pátio, Ribeira Brava

Seated at tables tucked into a maze of gardens and terraces, you can feast on simple, good-value grilled salmon, steaks or chicken. ◈ *Rua de São Bento 37 • Map D5 • 291 952 296 • €€*

Left **Santa Cruz** Right **Machico's fortress**

Eastern Madeira

MOST VISITORS CATCH A GLIMPSE OF EASTERN MADEIRA *as they arriv⋅ flying in over Machico, the island's second biggest town, and driving from the airport to Funchal along the south coast highway. Away from thes⋅ areas, there are wide expanses of untamed nature where no roads go. The⋅ include the whole north coast, with its exhilarating paths and vertigo-inducing cliffs. Also worth seeking out are the historic whaling village of Caniçal, the charming town of Santa Cruz and the gentle, pastoral landscape of the Santo da Serra plateau, source of the island's wicker products.*

Sights

1. Garajau
2. Caniço de Baixo
3. Santa Cruz
4. Machico
5. Caniçal
6. Ponta de São Lourenço
7. The Ilhas Desertas
8. Portela
9. Santo António da Serra
10. Camacha

Fishing boats on the beach at Caniçal

Garajau

A miniature version of Rio [de] Janeiro's statue of [Ch]rist the Redeemer [w]as erected on the [ba]ld and rocky headland [at] the southern end of [th]e village in 1927. The [fe]rns (*garajau* in Portuguese) [th]at gave their name to the [vil]lage can still be seen [fro]m the zigzag path that [wi]nds down the cliff face to [the] pebble beach below the [he]adland. Underwater [wa]ves and reefs rich in [m]arine life extend for [1]km (1 mile) to either [si]de, and are protected [as] a marine reserve *(see p90)*. ◈ *Map J6*

Statue of Christ the Redeemer, Garajau

Caniço de Baixo

Along Rua Baden Powell, the [m]ain street of this clifftop holiday [vil]lage, you will find Inn and Art [*(s]ee p115)*, a charming villa hotel [th]at mounts exhibitions of modern [ar]t. The tiny Praia da Canavieira [pu]blic beach is reached down an [ea]sily-missed alley near the [ju]nction with Rua da Falésia. For [a]small sum you can also use the [Ga]lomar Lido (open 9am–7pm [su]mmer, 10am–5pm winter). The [Lid]o is the base for the Manta [Di]ving Centre, which organizes [tri]ps to the Garajau Marine [Re]serve *(see above)*. ◈ *Map J6*

[Ga]lomar Lido, Caniço de Baixo

Santa Cruz

Santa Cruz is a town of great character, and surprisingly peaceful, given that the airport runway is right next door. The focal point is the beach, lined with cafés and *pastelarias* (pastry shops), as well as the Art Deco-style Palm Beach Lido, painted azure and cream. Back from the coast and down winding alleys is a 15th-century Gothic church as splendid as the cathedral in Funchal, and perhaps designed by the same architect *(see p8)*. ◈ *Map K5* • *SAM bus 20, 23, 53, 60, 70, 78, 113, 156*

Machico

Machico is where Captain Zarco and his crew first set foot on Madeira in 1420. The chapel they founded *(see p40)* is on the eastern side of the harbour, shaded by giant Indian fig trees. A statue of Machico's first governor, Tristão Vaz Teixeira, stands in front of the fine 15th-century parish church on the main square. A grid of cobbled alleys leads from here down to the seafront fortress. ◈ *Map K4* • *SAM bus 20, 23, 53, 78, 113, 156*

Caniçal

Caniçal holds the dubious honour of being a former whaling port. In 1956, John Huston came here to shoot the opening scenes of *Moby Dick*, but its star, Gregory Peck, became so seasick that they had to shoot the rest in a studio. The Museu da Baleia *(see p39)* explains how conservation has replaced whaling. Tuna fishing now plays a vital role in the local economy. ◈ *Map L4* • *SAM bus 113*

Volcanic cliffs at Ponta de São Lourenço

6 Ponta de São Lourenço

The long, narrow chain of eroded volcanic cliffs and ravines at the eastern tip of Madeira is an exciting and dramatic wilderness, protected as a nature reserve because of its coastal plants. The rocky peninsula can be explored from the much-used path that starts from the car park located at the end of the south coast road. ✹ Map M4

7 The Ilhas Desertas

Ponta de São Lourenço is linked underwater to the offshore Ilhas Desertas ("Desert Isles"), which form part of the same volcanic formation. Though arid and uninhabited, these islands nevertheless host all sorts of rare and endangered wildlife, including spiders, monk seals, petrels and shearwaters. An application has been made to UNESCO to have the islands declared a World Natural Heritage Site. For a closer look, contact one of the boat companies based at Funchal's marina, many of which offer day-long trips to the islands (see p52). ✹ Map J1

The Ilhas Selvagens

Also part of the Madeiran archipelago are the arid and treeless Ilhas Selvagens ("Wild Islands"), which lie 285 km (178 miles) south of Madeira and 165 km (103 miles) north of Tenerife, in the Canaries. These tiny volcanic islets, claimed by Portugal in 1458, have Europe's largest nesting colonies of rare shearwaters and storm-petrels. Since 1976, military sentries from the Nature Guards team have been permanently stationed on the islands to protect the birds, which were once caught, salted and dried as a delicacy.

8 Portela

The viewing point at Portela has more than its fair share of roadside cafés because it was once the transport hub for the east of the island. New tunnels linking São Roque do Faial with Machico have changed all that, but Portela is still an important landmark for walkers. You can walk south from here to Porto da Cruz (see p78) along a trail once used by wine carriers, or west along the Levada do Portela through dense primeval woodland and mountain scenery to Ribeiro Frio (see p76). ✹ Map J4 • SAM bus 53, 78

Santo António da Serra

The village of Santo António
Serra (known to Madeirans
ply as Santo da Serra), sits
the middle of a plateau flat
ough for golf courses (see
9) and fields of grazing cows.
spite its frequent cloud cover,
althy English merchants once
lt rural homes here: one of
former homes of the Blandy
nily (see p25) is now a public
k with camellias, hydrangeas
d rhododendrons, and viewing
nts that look out toward Ponta
São Lourenço. ◎ Map J4 •
ocarros da Camacha bus 77

Camacha

A monument in the centre
Camacha proudly declares
t Portugal's first ever game of
tball was played in the town
1875, organized by an English
oolboy. However, it is the
Relógio ("The Clock") wicker
tory opposite (see p56) that
ws people here, rather than
soccer history. You can see
monstrations of wicker-making
the workshop. If you explore
back streets of the village,
u can spot the raw material:
cks of freshly cut willow
es. These are steeped in
ter and stripped of their bark,
fore being boiled to make
m pliable enough to weave.
Map J5 • Autocarros da Camacha bus
77, 110

elógio wicker workshop, Camacha

A Day in Eastern Madeira

Morning

Assuming you are staying
in Funchal, start off by
getting onto the south
coast highway (follow
signs to the airport), then
take the São Gonçalo exit
and head for Camacha. The
road passes the Quinta do
Palheiro Ferreiro gardens
(see p24). **Camacha**
is famous for its wicker.
Head to the workshop
on the main square for an
insight into how they are
constructed (see p56).

Carry on to **Santo António
da Serra** for a walk in the
wooded park. Then continue
through the village and
turn left where the road
forks for **Machico** (see
p87), with its churches
and fortress. Depending
on the time, you might
want to stop in **Caniçal**
(see p87) for lunch and to
see the Museu da Baleia
(see p39), devoted to the
subject of whales.

Afternoon

About 3 km (2 miles) east
of Caniçal, you will reach a
car park marked "Prainha".
Follow the path down to
Madeira's only natural sand
beach, perfect for a swim.

At the mini-roundabout just
beyond the car park, turn
left and you will come to a
head-spinning viewpoint.
Back at the roundabout,
turn left again and continue
to a large car park. From
here, you can sample the
first part of the path that
leads across the treeless
peninsula to the east of the
island. Head back toward
Funchal and leave the south
coast highway at **Santa
Cruz** (see p87), where you
will find a good choice of
restaurants for dinner.

Bottle-nosed dolphins

Garajau Marine Reserve Sights

1 Monk Seal
Europe's most endangered mammal, the monk seal was once persecuted by Madeiran fishermen. The small surviving colony is now protected, but can be seen on trips to the Ilhas Desertas *(see pp52, 88)*.

2 Sperm Whale
Caniçal's fishermen caught their last sperm whale in 1981. This is the whale you are most likely to see on whale-watching trips *(see p52)*.

3 Humpback Whale
The humpback loves to leap out of the water and perform acrobatic somersaults (known as "breaching"). Madeirans can regularly spot this graceful whale offshore during the winter. A mere 20,000 remain in existence.

4 Pilot Whales
Large schools of pilot whales use Madeira as a migration route as they pass between the sub-tropical waters of the Canary Islands on their way north to the Arctic, though their precise route remains a mystery.

5 Killer Whales
Despite their name, these big whales (the largest members of the dolphin family) have never been known to attack humans – they are more likely to attack other whales. Solitary killer whales can often be spotted patrolling Madeira's warm waters.

6 Common Dolphin
No longer as common as their name suggests. Populatio numbers of these endangered mammals have bounced back, however, since the creation of Madeira's ocean marine reserv

7 Bottle-nosed Dolphin
The bottle-nosed dolphin is another sea mammal that has benefited from the creation of the reserve, which stretches 200,000 km sq (77,200 sq mile from eastern Madeira to the Ilhas Selvagens ("Wild Islands" a group of uninhabited rocks north of the Canary Islands.

8 Gulls
Herring gulls and western yellow-legged gulls are the seabirds you are most likely to see on boat trips or hanging around fishing ports such as Caniçal or Funchal.

9 Common Terns
Related to gulls, but with a deeply forked tail and a gracef flight, Common terns can be seen from the lookout point at Garajau, skimming the water a diving for small fish.

10 Shearwaters
The shearwater is able to glide just above the waves, scarcely moving its wings. On it was hunted by fishermen, w regarded it as a delicacy. Made has more than six varieties, including the Great Shearwate

Price Categories

For a three course meal for one with half a bottle of wine (or equivalent meal), taxes and extra charges.	**€** under €15
	€€ €15–€25
	€€€ €25–€40
	€€€€ €40–€60
	€€€€€ over €60

cado Velha, Machico

0 Places to Eat

California, Garajau
Welcoming restaurant with eerful yellow, white and blue cor, offering swordfish, beef oabs and scabbard fish as well salads and delicious desserts. *Opposite the Dom Pedro Hotel lap J6 • 291 933 935 • €€*

Pastipan, Santa Cruz
Pull up a chair, order a coffee, d choose from a wide selection delicious cheesecakes, egg stards and almond-based pastries this deservedly popular café on e Santa Cruz seafront. *Travessa Figueira • Map K5 • Closed Sun • €*

La Perla, Caniço de Baixo
Dishes such as seafood *otto au champagne* and fillet veal with rosemary are made ng organically-grown vege- oles from the garden. *Quinta endida Hotel, Estrada da Ponta Oliveira • Map J6 • 291 930 400 • €€€€*

Gallery, Caniço de Baixo
The Inn and Art hotel's rest- rant is a hit with vegetarians, whom there's a special dish the day and a range of salads. e fish is grilled on a eucalyptus od fire. *Rua Baden Powell 61/2 lap J6 • 291 938 200 • €€€*

A Brisa do Mar, Caniçal
This glass-fronted café serves icious *doses – tapas*-like dishes shrimp or stewed octopus. The acent restaurant grills fish fresh m the harbour. *Piscinas do içal • Map L4 • 291 960 700 • €€*

Bar Amarelo, Caniçal
Among the buildings of Caniçal, the cream-coloured limestone-and-steel decor of this harbourside gem stands out. Choose from salads, pasta or grilled fish. *Caniçal • Map L4 • 291 961 798 • Closed Wed • €€*

Mercado Velho, Machico
The courtyard of the old seafront market in Machico has been turned into an alfresco restaurant serving grilled fish and meat. *Rua do Mercado • Map K4 • 291 965 926 • €€*

O Relógio, Camacha
Come here on Friday or Saturday to see one of Madeira's top folk song-and-dance acts. As well as local dishes, there are specials, such as smoked fish, and grilled prawns in a chilli and garlic sauce. *Largo da Achada • Map J5 • €€*

Praia dos Reis Magos
This simplest of beachside restaurants within feet of the shore serves the local fishermen's daily catch. *Praia dos Reis Magos (1 km (half a mile) east of Caniço de Baixo) • Map J6 • 291 934 345 • €*

Miradouro de Portela, Portela
Homely restaurant in the style of a timber hunting lodge, with warming fires and generous portions of herb-flavoured beef kebabs and home-made cider. *Portela • Map J4 • 291 966 169 • €€*

Left **Porto Santo's beach** Right **Church of Nossa Senhora da Piedade, Vila Baleira**

Porto Santo

PORTO SANTO LIES *43 km (27 miles) northeast of Madeira. Zarco (see p* *and his crew took shelter here in 1418, while on their way to explore t* *west coast of Africa. Realizing that the island would be a useful base, he* *returned here in 1419 to plant the Portuguese flag, going on to Madeira t* *following year. Early settlers introduced rabbits and goats, which quickly* *stripped the island of its vegetation, so Porto Santo is not as green as* Madeira. Instead, the "Golden Island" has one major asset: its magnificent sandy beach, which brings holidaymakers from Madeira and mainland Europe in search of sunshine, sea and the agreeable sense of being a very long way from the busy world.*

🔟 Sights

1. The Beach
2. Vila Baleira
3. Nossa Senhora da Piedade
4. Casa Museu Cristóvão Colombo
5. The Jetty
6. Pico de Ana Ferreira
7. Ponta da Calheta
8. Zimbralinho
9. Fonte da Areia
10. Pico do Castelo

View from Ponta da Calheta, the island's westernmost point

Preceding pages **Typical tile picture on the building of the Portuguese Chamber of Commerce, Funchal**

e old town of Vila Baleira, capital of Porto Santo

1 The Beach

On top of Porto Santo's lcanic rocks, limestone, ndstone and coral were laid wn millions of years ago, neath a warm, shallow sea. lling sea levels exposed the ral to erosion, and the result the magnificent 10-km (6-mile) veep of sand that runs along e southern side of the island. icked by dunes and tamarisk ees, the beach is clean, wild d undeveloped, but bathers e never far from a beachside ifé. Enjoying the beach may ve therapeutic benefits: burying urself in the sand is said to ing relief from rheumatism d arthritis. ◈ *Map L2*

2 Vila Baleira

All life on the island centres the capital, which sits roughly lfway along the southern coast. ivement cafés fill the main uare, Largo do Pelourinho Pillory Square"), where fenders were once punished d public proclamations read out. ie town hall, with its double aircase flanked by dragon ees, now stands on the site of e pillory. The cobbled pavement front has a glass-topped, one-lined pit, which was once ied for storing grain. ◈ *Map L2*

3 Nossa Senhora da Piedade

To the east of the main square in Vila Baleira stands the majestic parish church, Nossa Senhora da Piedade, completed in 1446. Gothic rib-vaulting and rainwater spouts carved with human and animal heads have survived from this earlier church, which was torched by pirates, then rebuilt in 1667. The 17th-century altar painting of Christ being laid in his tomb is by Martím Conrado. The saints on either side were painted in 1945 by German artist Max Romer *(see p13)*. ◈ *Map L2*

4 Casa Museu Cristóvão Colombo

Christopher Columbus (1451– 1506) came to Madeira in 1478 as the agent for a Lisbon sugar merchant. Here he met and married Filipa Moniz, daughter of the governor of Porto Santo. Their son was born in 1479, but Filipa died soon after the birth, and Columbus left the islands in 1480. The house where he and Filipa are said to have lived is now a museum, displaying portraits of Columbus, maps of his voyages and models of his vessels.
◈ *Rua Cristóvão Colombo 12 • Map L2 • 291 983 405 • Open 10am–6pm Tue–Fri, 10am–1pm Sat & Sun • Free*

Casa Museu Cristóvão Colombo

For details of flights and ferries to Port Santo See p103

Water, Wine and Lime

Water, wine and lime were once Porto Santo's economic staples. Mineral water was bottled at the disused factory opposite the Torre Praia Hotel access road. Quicklime (used in mortar) made in lime kilns like the one at the Torre Praia was exported to Madeira and beyond. You can still buy Listrão Branco, the local fortified wine, but less is made every year.

The Seafront

5 The palm-lined path leading from the centre of Vila Baleira to the seafront is flanked by landscaped gardens dotted with rusty cannons. There are also memorials to Columbus (a bust set on a pedestal), to the 16th-century soldiers and sailors who colonized Madeira (an obelisk carved with abstract figures), and to the sailors who used to risk their lives crossing heavy seas to keep Porto Santo supplied with food and firewood (a bronze statue of a sailor at the rudder of a boat). Map L2

Pico de Ana Ferreira

6 Porto Santo consists of a saddle of land between two groups of cone-shaped volcanic

The rugged coastline and azure waters of Zimbralinho

peaks. At 283 m (929 ft), the Pico de Ana Ferreira is the highest of the summits at the more developed western end of the island. A road up its southern slopes will take you as far as the 17th-century Church São Pedro. From there, a track leads around the peak to a disused quarry featuring an interesting formation of prisma basalt columns aptly known as the "Organ Pipes". Map L2

Basalt structures on Pico de Ana Ferreira

Ponta da Calheta

7 The westernmost tip of the island is a beautiful spot, with a series of secluded sandy coves reached by scrambling over wave-eroded rocks. From the bar and restaurant at the end of the coast road, you can look across to Ilhéu de Baixo, the large, uninhabited rocky islet southwest of Porto Santo Madeira, too, is visible on the distant horizon, resembling a huge whale and usually capped by clouds. Map K2

Zimbralinho

8 Zimbralinho is the most beautiful of all the little rocky coves nestling along the western flank the island, its transparent blue seas popular with swimmers and divers. The cove is at its best around lunchtime, as it is shaded earlier and later in the day.

If you enjoy walking, buy the Guide to the Paths and Routes of the Island of Porto Santo *from local shops or the tourist office.*

…nd-eroded cliffs, Fonte da Areia

…he path to the cove starts at …e end of the road that leads to …e Centro Hipico, at the western …nd of the island. ◈ *Map K2*

⑨ Fonte da Areia

Water once bubbled straight …ut of the sandstone cliffs at …onte da Areia ("Fountain of …and"), but in 1843 the spring …as tamed, and you can now …ste the natural, rock-filtered …ineral water by simply turning a …p. The path to the spring leads …own a wind-eroded gully, where …e cliffs have been sculpted into …minated sheets of harder and …ofter rock. Lovers have carved …eir names on the rock face, but …o ferocious is the scouring wind …at declarations of perpetual …ve inscribed 10 years ago are …ow growing faint. ◈ *Map L1*

⑩ Pico do Castelo

The high peak to the east of …la Baleira is called Castle Peak, …ough despite its name, it was …ever fortified. From the 15th …entury on it was used as a …ace of refuge whenever pirates …reatened to attack. It was …quipped with a cannon, which …till survives at the lookout point …ear the summit. A cobbled road …kes you all the way to the …okout, past the cypress, cedar …d pine trees that have been …anted to turn the slopes from …ndy to green. ◈ *Map L1*

A Day on Porto Santo

Morning

🕐 You should ideally hire a car *(see p98)* for this tour, though you could do it by taxi. Start by driving north-east out of **Vila Baleira** *(see p95)*, up to the viewing point at Portela. Nearby, you will see three windmills of a type once common on Porto Santo. Carry on around the eastern end of the island, until a turning to the right takes you down to Serra de Fora beach. Some 2 km (1 mile) further north are traditional stone houses at Serra de Dentro and fine views from Pico Branco.

At the Camacha crossroads, a drivable track to the left leads up **Pico do Castelo**, soon turning into a stone-paved road. The viewing point at the top has great views over central Porto Santo. Back down at Camacha, there is a choice of cafés and bars for lunch.

Afternoon

First stop after lunch is **Fonte da Areia**. Despite looking arid, Porto Santo has several natural springs like this one. Next, head on toward Campo de Cima. As you drive alongside the airport runway, you will see some of the few vineyards left on the island that still produce wine.

Take the road up **Pico de Ana Ferreira**, then continue on foot to see its extraordinary-looking basalt columns. Afterwards, drive on to the stunning westernmost tip of the island, **Ponta da Calheta**. You should have plenty of time for relaxing on the sand, a swim, or a drink at the beach bar, before returning to Vila Baleira.

Left **Shopping at the Centro Artesanato** Right **Beachcombing**

TOP10 Activities

1 Sightseeing
Take a tour in an open-top bus to get a feel for the island. Two-hour tours depart daily at 2pm from the bus stop by the petrol station on the eastern side of the jetty. ◈ *Map L2*

2 Exploring by Car
Taxis offer reasonably priced island tours (around €15 per person), but if you prefer to explore independently, you can hire a car for the day from Moinho Rent-a-Car. ◈ *Map L2 • 291 983 260*

3 Exploring by Bike
Auto Acessórios Colombo (opposite the road to the Torre Praia Hotel) rents out bicycles and scooters. ◈ *Map L2 • 291 984 438*

4 Beachcombing
Take a leisurely stroll along the unbroken sands from Vila Baleira to Ponta da Calheta *(see p96)*. Tropical shells and the occasional bean-shaped seed (known as "Columbus Beans", because they are said to have inspired the explorer to look for land on the other side of the Atlantic) often wash up on the shore. ◈ *Map L2*

5 Watersports
Mar Dourado, located on the sands at Praia da Fontinha beach below the Torre Praia Hotel, rents out pedalos and kayaks, and will organize paragliding, waterskiing and boat trips. ◈ *Mar Dourado • 965 354 781 • Map L2*

6 Sailing
Sailing trips take you to otherwise inaccessible coves and islands at the westernmost end of Porto Santo for that much sought-after, tranquil feeling of being on your own desert island ◈ *Farwest Sailing Trips • Map L2 • 914 843 985*

7 Diving
Thanks to unpolluted seas and the absence of commercial fishing, Porto Santo's shores are rich in marine life. See for yourself with Porto Santo Sub, based at the marina. ◈ *Porto Santo Sub • Map L2 • 916 033 997*

8 Horse riding
Porto Santo's newly opened Centro Hípico (Equestrian Centre) takes beginners, and is located at Ponta, at the western end of the island. ◈ *Centro Hipico, Ponta • Map K2 • 291 983 258*

9 Golf
A brand-new 18-hole golf course – Porto Santo Golfe – has recently opened for business on the eastern flanks of the Pico do Ana Ferreira. ◈ *Map L2 • 291 983 778*

10 Shopping
Shells, model ships and other souvenirs with a nautical theme are the stock-in-trade of Port Santo's craft shops, which you will find located in the Centro do Artesanato, next to the jetty. ◈ *Map L2*

Left **Hotel Porto Santo** Right **Mar e Sol beach restaurant**

10 Places to Eat and Stay

1 Pé na Água, Vila Baleira
Not quite "foot in water" as the name suggests, but you are right by the sand at this board-walk spot. The chef cooks a great seafood rice, as well as grilled fish and beef kebabs. ⊗ Seafront, beyond the Torre Praia Hotel • Map L2 • 291 983 114 • €€

2 Mar e Sol, Vila Baleira
Grilled fish and *fragateira* (prawns, octopus, white fish and shellfish cooked with potatoes, onions and tomatoes) are popular at this beach terrace located by the Hotel Porto Santo. ⊗ Campo de Baixo • Map L2 • 291 982 269 • €€

3 O Calhetas, Calheta
The "Sunset Bar" has an enviable position at the western end of the island, where you can sip cocktails and enjoy garlic-rich *feijoada de mariscos* (prawns and clams with beans and tomatoes). ⊗ Map K2 • 291 984 380 • €€

4 Estrela do Norte, Camacha
The "Star of the North" is a *churrascaria* – a grill restaurant – set in a farmhouse in a northern village. Choose from locally sourced steak, tuna and octopus, or more pricey imported seafood. ⊗ Map L1 • 291 983 500 • €€

5 Baiana, Vila Baleira
Join the locals at this popular restaurant. Of the many fish caught daily, there's bound to be one you haven't tried. ⊗ Rua Dr Nuno Teixeira 9 • Map L2 • 291 984 649 • €€

6 Pizza N'Areia, Vila Baleira
Menus heavy on meat make life difficult for vegetarians here, so this restaurant serving pizzas and fresh salads is a blessing. ⊗ Rua Goulart Medeiros (part of the Torre Praia Hotel) • Map L2 • 291 980 450 • €

7 Porto Santo, Vila Baleira
Tucked almost invisibly into the dunes, this discrete hotel has long been the choice of visitors looking for a complete escape; at some times of day, the loudest sounds are the chirping of the sparrows in the lush green palm-shaded gardens. Mini-golf, gym, swimming pool and beachside bar. ⊗ Campo de Baixo • Map L2 • 291 980 140 • www.hotelportosanto.com • €€€

8 Torre Praia, Vila Baleira
With a cocktail bar in the tower, and an atrium built around a historic lime kiln, the Hotel Torre Praia has plenty of character. ⊗ Rua Goulart Medeiros • Map L2 • 291 980 450 • www.torrepraia.pt • €€€

9 Luamar ApartHotel, Cabeço da Ponta
Located 4 km (2 miles) west of Vila Baleira, the Luamar is the island's best self-catering choice. ⊗ Map L2 • 291 984 121 • www.luamar.net • €€

10 Pensão Central, Vila Baleira
The Central is a bright and friendly hotel whose only draw-back is the short climb from the town centre. ⊗ Rua Coronel A M Vasconcelos • Map L2 • 291 982 226 • €

For a guide to restaurant and hotel price ranges **See pp71 and 113 respectively**

STREETSMART

MADEIRA'S TOP 10

Left **Madeira tourist office** Right **Christmas, peak season on Madeira**

Top 10 General Information

1 When to Go
Christmas is peak season; hotels charge double their normal rates. Easter, July and August are also busy. June is surprisingly quiet, and enjoys perfect weather. Madeira has a generally mild sub-tropical climate, with average temperatures ranging from 17° C (62° F) in February to 23° C (75° F) in September. October to March sees the highest rainfall, especially on the northern side of the island. Porto Santo tends to be fine throughout the year.

2 What to Pack
Even in winter it is warm enough to eat out of doors during the day, so you will need light clothes, with extra layers for nights and the cooler mountains. Casual wear is the norm. If you intend to walk, bring a torch (flashlight), waterproofs and non-slip shoes.

3 Tourist Offices
The Portuguese tourist office has branches in most countries, but offers only basic information on Madeira. The Madeira tourist board's website is helpful, but infrequently updated. Funchal's main tourist office sells guides, maps, bus timetables and tickets for cultural events. ⊗
Madeira Board of Tourism: Avda Arriaga 16, Funchal. Map P3. 291 211 902. Open 9am–8pm Mon–Fri, 9am–6pm Sat & Sun. www.madeiratourism.org

4 Passports and Visas
Visitors can stay on Madeira for 90 days with a valid passport or recognized EU identity card and an onward or return ticket. There are no embassies on the island itself (they are all located in Lisbon). Several consulates are located in Funchal *(see box)*.

5 Customs
As part of the European Union, Madeira imposes virtually no restrictions on imports of cigarettes and alcohol from other EU member states, as long as they are for private consumption.

6 Public Holidays
Everything closes on 25 Dec, 1 Jan and throughout Easter. The following are also holidays: Shrove Tuesday, Ash Wednesday, 25 April, 1 May, Corpus Christi (June), 10 June, 1 July, 15 Aug, 21 Aug, 5 Oct, 1 Nov and 1 Dec. Shops and offices close on public holidays; large supermarkets stay open, as do businesses aimed at tourists.

7 Electricity and Water
The electricity supply is 220 volts AC. Sockets accept plugs with two round pins. Transformers are required for 110-volt devices, and adaptors for non-continental plugs. Tap water is safe to drink; mineral water is cheap and readily available.

8 Opening Hours
Shops trade from 9am–7pm on weekdays and from 9am–1pm on Saturdays. Large super markets stay open until 10pm every day. Banks are open weekdays from 8:30am–3pm. Most museums are shut from noon on Saturday until Tuesday; a few are open on Sunday mornings. Churches mainly open from 8am–noon and again from 4–7pm.

9 Time Differences
Madeira observes exactly the same time the UK, throughout the year. At noon on Madeira it is 7am in New York and 4am in Los Angeles.

10 Language
Most Madeirans can converse in English. Many can also manage some French and German phrases, in addition to their native Portuguese.

Consulates in Funchal

Belgium 291 210 200
France 291 200 750
Germany 291 220 338
Italy 291 223 890
Netherlands 291 223 830
Norway 291 741 515
Spain 962 381 599
Sweden 291 233 603
UK 291 212 860
USA 291 235 636

Preceding pages **Stalls at Funchal's Mercado dos Lavradores**

Cruise ship Right **Plane at Porto Santo's airport**

Getting to and Around Madeira

By Air From Europe

P Air Portugal operates scheduled flights (direct via Lisbon) from major European hubs, while new carriers (such as GB Airways) are entering the market. Online travel agents, including Expedia, are the quickest way to check flights and prices. Charter flights are cheaper, but may only be available as part of a package or for trips of a week's duration. ◈ TAP Air Portugal: www.tap-airportugal.co.uk (UK); www.tap-airportugal.us (USA) • GB Airways: www.gbairways.com

By Air From the Americas

As there are no direct flights from the US, you will fly into Lisbon, then continue on the 90-minute onward leg to Madeira.

Santa Catarina Airport

Funchal's airport is small and functional, with car hire, banking services and taxis, but little else. The airport bus departs for Funchal at roughly 90-minute intervals, but its schedules do not always coincide with incoming flights. ◈ Map • 291 520 700

Cruising

Madeira features on many cruise itineraries, but passengers rarely spend more than a few hours in port, so this is not a realistic option for experiencing the island.

Taxis

Madeira's yellow taxis are ubiquitous and relatively inexpensive. Drivers have to display a table of fixed charges (for trips such as that from the airport to Funchal), and must use their meters on other journeys. You can also use taxis for half- and whole-day tours of the island: make sure you agree a rate in advance (around €40 for a half day or €90 for a whole day).

Buses

Buses are an easy, economical way of getting around the island, though services are geared to the peak commuter hours of 8–10am and 4–7pm. The full timetable is available from the main tourist office. Tickets can be bought from the kiosks alongside bus stops or directly from drivers.

Car Rental

For the ultimate flexibility, hire a car. If you do this, however, you should be aware that parking in Funchal is very difficult – and metered. Underground car parks are the most convenient option. Local companies, such as Wind Car Rental and Amigos do Auto, can offer cheaper deals than international franchises. ◈ Wind Car Rental: 291 766 697 • Amigos do Auto: 291 776 726

Rules of the Road

Madeira's roads are improving, but be careful when you join a fast highway from a slip road. You may have difficulty getting above second gear on one of the island's older roads, which tend to be steep and winding. Parked cars, buses and pedestrians are everywhere, so drive with caution. If another driver flashes his lights, he is proceeding, not giving way.

Porto Santo by Air

Flights to Porto Santo from Santa Catarina Airport depart at one- or two-hour intervals throughout the day. The trip takes 15 minutes; you can check in up to 45 minutes before departure. Tickets can be booked through any travel agent or at the TAP Air Portugal office. They cost around €105 return. ◈ TAP Air Portugal: Avenida do Mar 8–10, Funchal. Map L2. 291 239 211

Porto Santo by Sea

The sea journey, by luxury cruise liner equipped with cinemas, restaurants, shops and games rooms, takes two-and-a-half hours. Ships leave Funchal at 8am, returning at about 10pm. Tickets can be booked through a travel agent, or bought at the port before boarding. The cost is around €75 return. ◈ Porto Santo Line: Rua da Praia 6, Funchal. Map Q3. 291 210 300

Left **Madeiran policeman** Right **Pharmacy**

TOP 10 Health and Security

1 Insurance
Make sure that you take out adequate travel insurance to cover yourself for private medical treatment, as well as for loss or theft of belongings. You should also be certain that your policy is valid for any holiday activities you might undertake, such as riding, scuba diving or waterskiing. If you plan to hire a car while you are on the island, it might also be advisable to take out personal liability cover for damage to rented vehicles.

2 EU Form E111
If you are an EU citizen, you are entitled to claim free emergency medical treatment, but you must obtain and complete a form E111 from a post office in advance of your trip. You usually have to pay for any medical treatment in the first instance, then reclaim costs later – so you must be sure to retain any receipts for medical expenses that you incur.

3 Bites and Stings
Mosquitoes are not a major problem on the island, and there are no poisonous snakes or insects. Stray dogs and so-called "guard dogs" can be a hazard, and some walkers carry dog dazers in order to protect themselves from any unwanted attention.

Treatment should be sought for dog bites, but there is no record of rabies on Madeira.

4 Sun Protection
It is easy to suffer sunburn on Madeira at any time of the year, especially as the effects of too much sun are not apparent until some time after exposure. Cover your head, neck, arms and legs if you are exposed to the sun, use sunscreen, and carry sufficient water to prevent dehydration.

5 Health Centres
If you do need medical help, you will receive both swift and attentive service by going to the nearest health centre – in Portuguese, Centro de Saúde. Such centres are found in every village and parish.

6 Pharmacies
Pharmacies – or farmácias – have staff trained to diagnose minor ailments and prescribe appropriate remedies. Every village has a late-opening pharmacy – and any pharmacies that do not open late will have a notice on the door directing you to one that does.

7 Spa Therapy
You don't have to be ill to benefit from the many spa therapies on offer in Madeira. This is especially true of Porto Santo, where all of the

larger hotels have ther. centres offering hydro-therapy, aromatherapy, skincare, detox and massage treatments. Ask your hotel to give you a recommendation

8 Crime
Madeira is still refreshingly safe and f from crime – including pickpocketing, vandalis and generally antisocia behaviour. Even so, it would be unwise to ten fate by being too carele lock all your valuables i a hotel safe, or keep the close when out and abc

9 Police
If you lose any valuables, and intend t make an insurance clai you will need to make official police report. Th main police station in Funchal is at Rua da Infância 28; the police telephone exchange ca be reached on 291 208 200. There are police posts in every town.

10 Vehicle Breakdown
There is no national breakdown service on Madeira, but car rental companies will give yo the emergency number of their own service.

Emergency Services

Fire, police and ambulance
112

Bank of Portugal Right **Telephone kiosk**

Banking and Communications

Currency
Madeira uses the [euro]. Because of forgery, notes tend to be [tre]ated with suspicion, [so] ask for a mix of €50, [€20] and €10 notes when [cha]nging money.

Exchange
Banks in Madeira [can] be found in every [tow]n, and nearly all have [an] exchange service for [wh]ich they charge a [min]imum fee no matter [how] large or small the [tran]saction, so it is a [goo]d idea to change [larg]er amounts at a time. [Su]ch charges apply to [trav]eller's cheques, as [wel]l as transactions with [cas]h. Take your passport [whe]n you when you [cha]nge money. Banks [ope]n 8:30am–3pm [Mo]nday to Friday, though [som]e also open on [Sat]urday until 1pm.

Cash Machines
[Ne]arly all banks also [hav]e a hole-in-the-wall [cas]h machine that you [can] use to obtain euros [usi]ng a card that is part [of] the Visa or Mastercard [net]work and your PIN [num]ber. Such transactions [ma]y be subject to an [adm]inistration fee and [to] interest payments [cha]rged by your own [car]d company.

Credit Cards
[The]oretically, credit [car]ds are accepted in [mo]st shops, as well as [the] more upmarket

restaurants, but most businesses prefer cash. As a result you may be given the excuse that there is a problem with your card, or told that it is not compatible with the system in Madeira, which, for most cards, requires you to key a PIN number into a keypad.

Public Phones
Card-operated phones are found in most town and village centres. Cards can be purchased from most newsagents, as well as supermarkets, and offer the cheapest way of calling home. To phone abroad, dial the international access code (00) and the country code (UK 44, US 1), then the area code without the initial zero, and finally the actual number.

Mobile Phones
Mobile coverage on Madeira is good, but the dialling rules differ from network to network, so check with your service provider before you go what codes you need to use to call someone from Madeira or for someone to call you.

Post Offices
Every town has a post office *(correios)*. Funchal's most central post office is on Avenida Zarco (8:30am–8pm Mon–Fri, 9am–1pm Sat). Poste restante services are available at the main post

office on Avenida Calouste Gulbenkian (same hours). Correspondence should be marked "Poste Restante", and you will need your passport to collect mail. Stamps can be purchased from most places that sell postcards.

Internet
Madeira is no stranger to cyberspace. Many hotels offer free webmail and internet access to their guests. Funchal has a number of internet cafés offering fast connections, printers, scanners, fax, café service and multilingual staff; they include Cyber Café, Global Net Café and Lidonet Internet. Ⓢ *Cyber Café: Avenida do Infante 6. Map Q1 • Global Net Café: Rua do Hospital Velho 25. Map P4 • Lidonet Internet: Monumental Lido Shopping Centre, shop 14. Map G6*

Television
Most hotels subscribe to the standard package of 30 satellite channels available on Madeira, including programmes in most European languages, plus MTV, CNN and BBC World. Reception tends to be somewhat variable outside Funchal.

Newspapers
Most newsagents in Funchal stock copies of the international editions of the main European daily newspapers, usually a day after publication.

The area code for Madeira and Porto Santo is 291. This number has to be dialled even when you are in Madeira or Porto Santo.

Left **Dolphin-watching yacht, Funchal** Right **Botanical Gardens, Funchal**

🔟 Specialist Holidays

1 Fly/Drive
You can experience Madeira to the full by using rural hotels as bases for walks and tours. The leading operators are Style Holidays and Caravela Tours in the UK; and Abreu Tours and Portugal Online in the US. Ⓢ www.style-holidays.co.uk
• www.caravela.co.uk
• www.abreu-tours.com
• www.portugal.com

2 Walking
Booking yourself on an organized walking tour means that everything is done for you, including ferrying your luggage around – all you have to do is enjoy the scenery. Ⓢ www.headwater.com
• www.exodus.co.uk
• www.discoverytravel.co.uk
• www.hfholidays.co.uk •
www.ramblersholidays.co.uk

3 Parks and Gardens
The advantage of a specialist holiday is that you get to see some of Madeira's private gardens – rich depositories of rare plants – as well as visiting public gardens in the company of an expert. Ⓢ www.brightwaterholidays.com • www.cachet-travel.co.uk • www.coxandkings.co.uk

4 Golf Packages
The Estalagem Serra Golf (see p115) and the Casa Velha do Palheiro (see p113) both offer golf packages with discounted green fees, guaranteed tee times, clinics and one-to-one lessons at all

levels. If your partner does not play, both hotels are well placed for visiting gardens and *levadas*.

5 Wildlife
From kiosks at Funchal's marina, several yacht charter companies organize expeditions to see the bird and marine life of Madeira's cliffs and islands, including dolphin- and whale-watching trips. Ⓢ Bonita da Madeira: 291 762 218 • Ventura do Mar: 291 280 033 • Albatroz: 291 223 366 • Gavião Madeira: 291 241 124

6 Fishing
Madeira's waters teem with big-game fish, including blue and white marlin, big-eye and blue-fin tuna, albacore and bonito. TuriMar, based at Funchal's marina, offers full- and half-day trips with equipment provided. It is a signatory to the tag-and-release scheme, whereby fish, once caught and photographed, are returned to the wild. Ⓢ TuriMar: 291 226 720

7 Diving
Just under the surface along Madeira's southern cliffs is a protected world of marine caves, colourful fish and crabs, sea urchins, corals and weeds that are invisible unless you know how to dive. Two hotels have permanent diving schools: Manta Diving is at the Galomar (see p115) in Caniço and Dive College

International is at the D Pedro in Machico. Ⓢ Manta Diving: www.ma diving.com • Dive Colleg International: 291 969 5

8 Adventure
Madeira is being discovered as an ideal destination for a range adventure sports, from mountain biking and r climbing to windsurfin surfing and paragliding Ⓢ Terras de Aventura: www.terrasdeaventura.c

9 Spa Holidays
Several hotels hav large spa complexes offering stress reducti and health and beauty facilities. These includ the Choupana Hills Res and Spa (see p113), th Thalassotherapy Spa a the Crowne Plaza (see p112), the Vital Centre the Jardim Atlântico (s p116), the Active Cent at the Maderia Palacio (see p115), the Phyton Health Spa at the Savo (see p112) and the Spa the Porto Mare (see p1

10 Honeymoons a Romantic Break
Many of Madeira's graceful old manor hou hotels reserve their fin rooms for honeymoone or those celebrating a special anniversary. The island's scenery and sunsets, as well as its indulgent pool and spa complexes, make for a memorable holiday. Ⓢ www.classic-collection.cc
• www.cadoganholidays.c

Walking along the Levada do Risco **Right** Madeiran bus

0 Walking Tips

Give it a Go
Many walkers rate [Ma]deira as one of the [be]st rewarding European [de]stinations and visit the [isl]and regularly. Find out [b]y walking on Madeira [ca]n be so addictive by [tak]ing a short walk on [yo]ur own, or by signing [up] for a guided walking [tou]r (see p51).

Maps and Guides
Madeira is changing [so] fast that no map or [gui]de is fully up-to-date. [The] ers of Sunflower [Bo]oks' Madeira walking [gui]de are extremely good [at p]roviding feedback [on] the latest changes, [wh]ich are posted on the [pub]lisher's website. ◎ [ww]w.sunflowerbooks.co.uk

Mountains or Woods
[Eve]ryone likes variety, [bu]t there are those who [op]t for mountain walks [an]d others who prefer a [w]oodland stroll. Madeira [cat]ers to both, with steep [co]bbled paths linking [th]e peaks of the island's [ce]ntral mountain range, [wh]ere vegetation is [sp]arse, and levada paths [th]at follow the contours [thr]ough more gentle, [do]mesticated landscapes.

Be Prepared
[3] Check a reliable guide [to] see what hazards you [ca]n expect on the route [an]d prepare accordingly. [Mo]untain walks lack [sh]ade and are susceptible [to] sudden downpours or chilly clouds that obscure the way ahead. Levada walks can be muddy and may involve long tunnels, waterfalls that cascade over the path or streams that have to be waded.

Choosing a Base
5 If you have come to Madeira just to walk, Funchal might not be the best place to stay. You may prefer to choose a hotel that is closer to a good choice of routes, such as the Pousada dos Vinháticos (see p116), the Residencial Encumeada (see p116) or the Solar de Boaventura (see p115).

Cars and Taxis
6 There are very few circular walks on Madeira. Fortunately, you can arrange to be dropped off and collected by taxi, or you can call a cab once you reach the end of your walk. Another option is to drive to the starting point of your walk, and take a taxi back to your car at the end.

Buses
7 A good walking guide will provide details of bus connections as well as a timing guide, so that you can see in advance how long each route will take. Madeira's rural buses are reliable, but on long-distance routes across the island there is only one bus a day, so you might have to get to the start of the walk by bus and return by taxi, or vice versa.

Mobile Phones
8 Mobile phones can be a pest, but they may also be a life-saver when used to call for help in an emergency. They are also useful simply for letting your taxi driver know how long you will be. If you do not have a mobile phone, let your hotel know where you are going and at what time you are due back, so that someone can raise the alarm if you fail to return.

Field Guide
9 Nothing can be more annoying than not being able to put a name to all the flowers, ferns, succulents and lichens that you will see along the route. Consider investing in a wildlife guide, such as Madeira's Natural History in a Nutshell by Peter Sziemer, available at most Funchal bookshops (see p57). Rather heavier than its title implies, it will tell you all you need to know about the island's geology, flora and fauna.

Picnics
10 Don't forget to pack a picnic to enjoy in a sunny glade or at a panoramic viewing point along your route. Any left-over crumbs of bread can be fed to the birds that will come to see what you are up to, or to the trout (escapees from local trout farms) that you may spot in some of the island's rivers and levadas.

Left **Royal Savoy pool complex** Right **View from Quinta Bela de São Tiago**

TOP 10 Accommodation Tips

1 Price and Location

On Madeira, location has a big influence on price. City-centre hotels tend to be cheap. The luxurious five-star hotels with sea views, along the Estrada Monumental to the west of the city, command the highest prices. Further west, in the hotel zone, prices fall the further you go from the city centre and from the sea.

2 A Room with a View

Some hotels have been designed so that every room looks out over the sea. Where this is not the case, you will find that you pay significantly more for a room with a sea view, especially if it has a sunny, south-facing balcony.

3 Beware of Noise

If you are sensitive to noise, make sure that you tell the hotel. Some rooms with so-called "mountain views" actually look out onto one of the island's busiest roads, the Estrada Monumental. You may also have trouble with noise if your room is located above the hotel restaurant, especially if it has live music or a disco.

4 Grading Systems

Madeira's grading system is a fairly accurate guide to the facilities you can expect. All four- and five-star (and most three-star) hotels offer heating, air-conditioning, television,

direct-dial telephone, a garage or parking facilities, a restaurant and a bar. The star grading system is not, however, a measure of service, ambience, character or quality.

5 Quintas and Estalagens

Estalagens (inns) or *quintas* (manor houses) are usually hotels of some age and historic character, often set on an estate with mature trees and fine gardens. In most cases, the bar, dining room and lounges are located in the old house, while guest rooms may be in modern blocks in the grounds.

6 Rural Tourism and Country Hotels

Farmers and landowners on Madeira are being encouraged to convert redundant agricultural buildings into cottages. To find one, look for green signs with the words *Turismo Rural*, ask at local tourist offices or check out Madeira's rural tourism website, through which you can book some 20 such properties around the island. ✪ *www.madeira-rural.com*

7 Children

Most hotel rooms are designed for double occupancy, but you are welcome to ask for an extra bed or two for children. Some hotels have family rooms that sleep four to six people.

8 Peak Seasons

Madeira is popular with Portuguese escap the summer heat of th mainland, so hotels te to be busy during July and August, when it is best to book well ahea Other popular times ar Christmas and New Ye the Carnival and Flowe Festival, and the week before, during and afte Easter. At all these times, room rates can be double the norm.

9 Winter Breaks

You can secure so exceptional bargains b visiting Madeira betwe November and March, when even Reid's Pala has been known to off discounts. Look out fo offers in newspaper tra supplements, or check with Madeira specialist ✪ *Strawberry World: www.madeira-portugal.c • www.destination-portu co.uk • www.saga.co.uk • www.travellersway.co.u*

10 Breakfast and Half-Board

Hotel prices on Madeir usually include a buffet breakfast (cereals, fres fruit, juices, pastries, cooked meats, cheese tea and coffee). Cooke breakfast is an option a deluxe hotels. Opting f half-board, with dinner the hotel restaurant, ca be good value, though your choice may be limited to just two dish per course, rather than the full à la carte menu

Expensive taxis Right **Charter flight at Funchal's airport**

Madeira on a Budget

Book Ahead and Online

...deira can be very ...eap. In fact the biggest ...st will be getting to ...e island, since the "no-...s" carriers don't serve ...and scheduled flights ...e rarely discounted, ...e to the high demand. ...e best way to secure a ...count is to book at ...st three months in ...vance, using an online ...ent such as Expedia.

Be Flexible

The best discounts ...e had by those who are ...xible about their travel ...tes and don't mind ...ng early in the morning ...late at night. Online ...ents show seat costs ...different flights and ...ow you to choose the ...eapest. The downside ...that, once booked, ...counted tickets cannot ...changed without ...ying a hefty penalty.

Charter Flights

UK charter airlines ...ch as Air 2000, Airtours, ...tannia, Excel, JMC ...d Monarch can offer ...e cheapest way to get ...Madeira, but many of ...em only offer flights ...re between April and ...tober. You may also ...d that they only fly ...ce a week, so a short ...eak is not an option.

Packages

Madeira's hotels are ...en not responsive to ...quests for a room ...scount, even when

they are quiet. The best way to secure a cheap deal is to book an inclusive package (including flights, room, meals, transfers, car hire and excursions) online or through an agent.

5 Last-minute Bargains

If you can travel at a week or two's notice, check travel agents' windows and advertised last-minute bargains. In some cases, you will not know where you are staying until you arrive, but bad hotels are rare on Madeira (and noise nuisance is more likely than a safety or hygiene problem).

6 Accommodation

Madeira has some astonishingly cheap accommodation in the city centre and at rural *pensions (see p117)*. Clean rooms with a shared bathroom are available for €15 to €25 a night, and even luxurious apartments can be had for €40 a night, if you are staying for a week or more. www.madeira-island.com has a useful accommodation section, which has links to the websites of several of Madeira's cheaper hotels.

7 Food

Madeira has literally hundreds of cheap cafés and restaurants, where you can eat very well for €10 a head by choosing simple dishes, such as

grilled sardines and salad. Better still, shop in local markets and supermarkets. Delicious bread, olives, fresh fruit and salad ingredients are all inexpensive, as well as ready-cooked dishes such as grilled chicken or beef-and-bean stew.

8 Transport

Avoid taxis and you will save money. You may have to wait up to an hour for the airport bus into Funchal, but it costs a few euros, compared with a minimum taxi fare of €20. Using buses to travel around the island will only cost a few euros, whereas a taxi will set you back ten times as much.

9 Guided Tours

Guided tours offer another cost-saving alternative to taxis or car hire. The downside is that you are forced to travel in a large group of people, and the trip may well include shop and restaurant stops that you might not want to make.

10 Bars and Entertainment

You can easily save money by avoiding discos and other nightlife venues where prices for drinks are several times higher than in ordinary bars. In the same way, a coffee or a glass of Madeira in a local bar will cost a third of the price of the same drink in your hotel bar.

Left **Flower stall** Right **Vintage Madeira wine**

TOP 10 Shopping Tips

1 Duty Free
Prices in Madeira airport's duty free shop are generally more expensive than in downtown wine shops and supermarkets. However, non-EU residents are entitled to a VAT refund.

2 Embroidery
Make sure that you don't pay high prices for cheap, machine-made embroidery imported from Asia, if what you are after is the genuine local article. All Madeiran embroidery is checked for quality before being passed for sale. It is marked with a hologram tag – and in some cases by a lead seal.

3 Non-vintage Wines
If you want to taste and buy quality Madeira wine (see p59), make sure the label mentions Sercial, Verdelho, Bual or Malvasia. This shows that the wine is of high quality and made by traditional methods, using the classic grape varieties. Wines labelled dry, medium dry, medium sweet or rich are massproduced and lack the subtlety and complexity of the best Madeira.

4 Aguardente
Another souvenir with a long history is aguardente (sugar cane spirit), often described as "rum". White aguardente lacks subtlety and is commonly served as poncha, mixed with lemon and honey. Aged, dark aguardente is a different matter entirely – an afterdinner drink with real character and flavour.

5 Leather Bargains
Prices on Madeira are generally higher than those found elsewhere in Europe because of the cost of importing goods to the island. The exceptions to this rule are shoes and leather goods, which are Portuguese specialities. There are plenty of leather shops to browse in along the narrow streets around the cathedral in Funchal (see pp8–9).

6 Flowers
To make sure that your flowers are as fresh as possible, and that they survive the journey home, ask the florist to deliver them to your hotel on the morning of your departure, packed in a robust cardboard container. Strelitzias (bird-of-paradise flowers) are especially popular because they last a long time: you can rely on enjoying them for up to a month or more.

7 Bolo de Mel
Another popular and long-lasting choice of souvenir is Madeiran Christmas cake, now made and sold all year round. Called bolo de mel (honey cake), it is a traditional cake made to a recipe that includes sugar cane syrup and spices and is an excell teatime treat.

8 Shopping Centr
Though they are threatening to drive th island's small shopkeepers out of busines there is no doubt that sheer choice and varie the best places to sho in Funchal are the large shopping centres. Amo the main ones are the Marina Shopping Cent and Madeira Shopping (see p69). Huge new centres are also planne for the hotel zone (Madeira Forum) and downtown Funchal.

9 Supermarkets
Large supermarket can also be good for souvenir hunting. Try th one at the Anadia Cent opposite the Farmers' Market in Funchal, or the one at the Lido, in the centre of the hotel zone. The supermarket chain Pingo Doce is als worth trying.

10 Scrimshaws
A word of warning: you may see carved whalebone ivory for sa in Caniçal and in the ca park at Ponta de São Lourenço. The trade is relic of the days when this region of Madeira had a whaling fleet. Do not be tempted to buy: taking whalebone products out of the country is illegal.

Unofficial tourist information centre **Right Trawling for custom outside of a restaurant**

0 Things to Avoid

1 Overcharging by Taxi Drivers

Taxi drivers very often take advantage of naive visitors by overcharging, especially on the journey to and from the airport. The government fixes the price for this trip usually. Taxi drivers are legally obliged to display a table of fixed fares and must use their meters for other journeys, unless you have agreed a price in advance.

2 Timeshare Touts

The problem is not as bad as in some other holiday resorts, but timeshare touts do operate in Funchal, accosting people on Avenida do Infante as they stroll into downtown Funchal from the hotel zone. If somebody greets you with a cheery "Hello, do you speak English?", there's a good chance that he's a tout. They are very persistent, so just answer with a polite "no, thank you".

3 Restaurant Touts

Restaurant touts are more difficult to shake off than the timeshare variety. They operate especially in the Zone Velha (Old Town), the marina complex and the restaurant strip along Caminho da Casa Branca. If you want to browse menus before choosing where to eat, it is best to do this in the morning or afternoon, avoiding times when restaurants trawl for customers.

4 Lobster

Remember that the oh-so-tempting "fresh lobster" much touted in seafood restaurants could end up costing you a small fortune. Lobsters are imported and priced by weight, so make sure you know exactly how much you will be charged.

5 Information Centres

Various establishments along the route from the hotel zone to downtown Funchal call themselves "tourist information centres" and offer free maps. In reality, they are tour agents that will extol the delights of Madeira in order to sign you up on a guided tour.

6 Guided Tours

Scores of tour companies offer identical trips in air-conditioned coaches. These are a good way of getting a quick overview of Madeira, but they involve compulsory shopping and restaurant stops. To gain a more personal view of the island, choose a mini-bus tour or ask your hotel to recommend a taxi driver who speaks English.

7 Aggressive Drivers

If you are thinking of hiring a taxi for a day or half-day trip, make sure the driver knows that fast driving and daredevil overtaking do not impress you. Aggressive driving is particularly dangerous on Madeira's narrow, twisting roads; it also leads rapidly to car sickness.

8 Hidden Car Costs

If you decide to hire a car and want to compare prices, don't be guided by the advertised daily rates. Make sure there are no hidden extras, such as tax and insurance, which can add 20 per cent or more to the basic daily rate.

9 Out-of-date Maps

Once you have your car, you might well want a map or a walking guide. Beware: most of the maps and guides sold in souvenir shops are years out of date, and can be seriously misleading, given how much Madeira has developed in recent years. Choose a reliable bookshop (see p57) and check the publication date before you buy.

10 Beggars

Although tourists come for the quaint boat-yard and pretty seaside setting of Câmara de Lobos (see p75), this fishing village also offers a glimpse of real life in Madeira. It is not unusual to see children begging for a couple of euros here. How you respond is up to you – but if you decide to give money be aware that it may encourage other children to approach you.

Left **Reid's Palace interior** Right **Noble Room, Savoy Hotel**

TOP 10 Character Hotels in Funchal

1 Reid's Palace
Truly one of the great hotels of the world, Reid's has the feel of a country house – genuine antiques and works of art at every turn, gardens dotted with pools and shady retreats, panoramic views, and some of Madeira's best restaurants *(see p60)*. ⊗ *Estrada Monumental 139 • Map H6 • 291 717 171 • www.reidspalace.com • €€€€€*

2 Savoy Classic
The Savoy is now two hotels in one. The original (Savoy Classic), where Margaret Thatcher spent her honeymoon, is linked to its sister (Savoy Royal) by a bridge. Guests at the Classic may also use the facilities of the Royal. ⊗ *Avenida do Infante • Map H6 • 291 213 000 • www.savoyresort.com • €€€€€*

3 Savoy Royal
The modern Savoy is a veritable museum of art and antiquities from all the parts of the world that Portuguese sailors ventured to during the 15th-century Age of Discovery. But the hotel's popularity with readers of the British *Daily Telegraph* newspaper (who voted it "second best resort hotel in the world") has more to do with its stunningly designed pool area, and the delicious fruit cocktails at the submerged bar. ⊗ *Rua Carvalho Araújo • Map H6 • 291 213 500 • www.savoyresort.com • €€€€€*

4 Crowne Plaza
Everything about the Crowne Plaza says "style", but this is also a hotel that cares about its guests, as its 24-hour gym, pool, squash courts, spa and crèche attest. ⊗ *Estrada Monumental 175/177 • Map G6 • 291 717 700 • www.madeira.crowneplaza.com • €€€€*

5 Cliff Bay
The Cliff Bay shares its prime position on the clifftops immediately west of Funchal with Reid's, the Savoy and the Crowne Plaza. A series of terraced gardens leads to palm-shaded swimming pools. Enjoy Italian food with spectacular harbour views in the Il Gallo d'Oro restaurant. ⊗ *Estrada Monumental 147 • Map G6 • 291 707 700 • www.portobay.com • €€€€*

6 Porto Mare
The Porto Mare is part of a stunning new resort hotel with wonderful gardens, a huge outdoor swimming pool, indoor pools, spa complex, children's crèche and gym, and a restaurant serving adventurous Mediterranean cuisine. ⊗ *Rua do Gorgulho 2 • Map G6 • 291 703 700 • www.portobay.com • €€€€*

7 Tivoli Ocean Park
Resembling a huge liner, the Tivoli Ocean Park looks out onto a lovely part of the Madeiran coast. The Boca do Cais is one of the island's best restaurants *(see p61)*. Children aged 5 to 12 h their own pool and Dolp Club with daily activitie ⊗ *Rua Simplício dos Pas Gouveia 29 • Map G6 • 2 702 000 • www.tivoliho com • €€€€*

8 Quinta da Casa Branca
"Where is the hotel?", are tempted to ask on arrival. The ultra-mode rooms in this imaginati designed complex are cleverly integrated into garden so as to be alm invisible, while providi guests with uninterrup views across green lav and shrub-filled borders ⊗ *Rua da Casa Branca 5 • Map G6 • 291 700 770 www.quintacasabranca.p • €€€€*

9 Quinta da Penha de França
This charming hotel is the best central budge choice. The busy worlo only intrudes when usin the footbridge to access the pool and sea platfo ⊗ *Rua Imperatriz Dona Amélia 87 • Map H6 • 29 204 650 • www.hotelquin penhafranca.com • €€*

10 Pestana Grand
This spacious new hotel has a large outdo pool and health centre. Eat Portuguese, Italian or Moroccan before enjoying the evening's entertainment. ⊗ *Rua Ponta da Cruz 23 • Map G6 • 291 707 400 • www.pestana.com • €€€*

Note: *Unless otherwise stated, all hotels accept credit cards, and have en-suite bathrooms and air conditioning*

Choupana Hills Resort

Price Categories

For a standard, double room per night (with breakfast if included), taxes and extra charges.

€ under €50
€€ €50–100
€€€ €100–150
€€€€ €150–200
€€€€€ over €200

Character Hotels beyond Funchal

Choupana Hills Resort and Spa, Funchal

A stunning complex of bungalows of wood, stone and tile, high up in the menthol-scented eucalyptus forest above Funchal. Enjoy a few days of pampering – complete with massage and spa treatments, and a fine restaurant, the Xôpana (see p61). ❂ Travessa do Largo da Choupana • Map G5 • 291 206 020 • www. choupanahills.com • €€€€€

Casa Velha do Palheiro, São Gonçalo

Built as a hunting lodge for the Count of Carvalhal, the 200-year-old Casa Velha serves some of the best food on the island (see p61). The Palheiro gardens (see pp24–5) are just over the hedge; Palheiro Golf (see p48) is at the end of the drive. ❂ Rua da Estalagem 23 • Map G6 • 291 790 350 • www. casa-velha.com • €€€€

Quinta do Monte, Monte

An oasis of calm, set high above Funchal in a lush, walled garden threaded by meandering cobbled paths. The manor at the heart of the estate is decorated with antique furniture and oriental rugs. The dining room (see p60) is set in a modern conservatory. ❂ Caminho do Monte 182 • Map H5 • 291 780 100 • www.charming hotelsmadeira.com • €€€

Quinta do Jardim da Serra, Jardim da Serra

This newly restored boutique hotel, with pool and health centre, is set in renowned gardens. The estate was founded by Henry Veitch (1782–1857), a wealthy Scottish entrepreneur who made a fortune supplying wine to the Portuguese navy. ❂ Fonte Frade • Map G6 • 291 911 500 • www.quintajardim daserra.com • €€€€

Quinta Splendida, Caniço

The Quinta Splendida describes its walled estate as a "botanical garden", because of its rare and beautiful planting, now enhanced by herb, fruit and vegetable gardens which supply the hotel kitchens. ❂ Estrada da Ponta Oliveira 11 • Map J5 • 291 930 400 • www.hotel quintasplendida.com • €€€

Quinta da Bela Vista, Funchal

The "Beautiful View" is of the wild cliffs to the east, but it could equally be describing the lovely gardens of this traditional manor house. ❂ Caminho do Avista Navios 4 • Map G6 • 291 706 400 • www. belavistamadeira.com • €€€€

Jardins do Lago, Funchal

This charming manor house set in six acres of gardens has a famous resident – a giant tortoise called Columbo. Rooms enjoy southerly views over the city. Features include a pool, tennis court, spa suite, billiards room and restaurant. ❂ Rua Dr João Lemos Gomes 29 • Map H5 • 291 750 100 • www. jardins-lago.com • €€€€

Quintinha de São João, Funchal

Set in an elegant suburb of Funchal, the Quintinha de São João has modern wings extending from its historic core. Facilities include outdoor pool, tennis court, sauna and well regarded restaurant. ❂ Rua da Levada de São João 4 • Map H5 • 291 740 920 • www.quintinhasao joao.com • €€€

Madeira Palacio, Funchal

The Madeira Palace keeps guests busy with a new health club, large outdoor and indoor pools, floodlit tennis courts, live music and a varied programme of night-time entertainment. ❂ Estrada Monumental 265 • Map G6 • 291 702 702 • www.hotel madeirapalacio.com • €€€€

Quinta das Vistas, Funchal

This 1930s-style hotel set high above the city has something of a colonial air, with palm-fringed public rooms, gardens and a veranda for alfresco dining. Pool, gym and spa. ❂ Caminho de Santo António 52 • Map G5 • 291 750 007 • www.charming hotelsmadeira.com • €€€€

For hotels on Porto Santo See p99

Left **Quinta Bela São Tiago** room Right **Residencial Santa Clara**

🔟 City-centre Hotels in Funchal

1 Quinta Bela São Tiago

Birdsong and tranquil gardens make you wonder whether you really are just a five-minute stroll from the busy heart of Funchal. Rooms – some of them huge – have views of the onion-domed church towers and terracotta roofs of the Zona Velha (Old Town). Outdoor pool and gym. ◈ *Rua Bela de São Tiago 70 • Map P6 • 291 204 500 • www.hotel-qta-bela-s-tiago.com • €€€€*

2 Porto Santa Maria

Built on the site of the city's former shipyard, the hotel overlooks Funchal's seafront promenade and is centrally located for shopping and restaurants. Two pools and health club. ◈ *Avenida do Mar 50 • Map Q5 • 291 206 700 • www.portobay.com • €€€€*

3 Quinta Perestrello

Set in mature gardens, this 150-year-old heritage hotel is a fine example of the elegant houses built by Madeiran merchants. Most of the rooms are in the old building – those at the back are quietest. Swimming pool. ◈ *Rua do Dr Pita 3 • Map G6 • 291 706 700 • www.charming hotelsmadeira.com • €€€*

4 Pestana Casino Park

If you want nightlife and entertainment, a stay at this huge 1960s hotel is as good as it gets, with a full programme of dinner dances and professional cabaret. The Copacabana Nightclub and the Madeira Casino are part of the complex. Gym, sauna, pool, tennis courts. ◈ *Rua Imperatriz Dona Amélia 55 • Map Q1 • 291 209 100 • www.pestana.com • €€€€*

5 Quinta do Sol

The Quinta do Sol is next to a busy road, but it has rooms overlooking the quiet green gardens of the Quinta Magnólia to the rear, or the hotel's own pool terrace. Many guests return – a credit to the friendliness of the staff. Live music and regular folklore performances. ◈ *Rua do Dr Pita 6 • Map H6 • 291 707 010 • www.enotel. com • €€€*

6 Windsor

This good-value hotel is popular with those who like to be in the midst of the bustle of the real Funchal, and don't need a gym or lots of restaurants (though there is a tiny pool on the roof). It scores by having friendly staff and a garage (parking in Funchal is very difficult). ◈ *Rua das Hortas 4C • Map P4 • 291 233 083 • www.hotel windsorgroup.com • €€*

7 Residencial Gordon

Located in the quietest of backstreets almost next door to the lovely grounds of the English Church, this cheap, plainly decorated hotel is a wonderful re-treat for no-frills travellers. No English is spoken, book with the help of Portuguese speaker. ◈ *Rua do Quebra Costas 3 • Map N1 • 291 742 366*

8 Residencial San Clara

A house of real charm with almost as many c as guests, and a cobb garden with a tiny cree hung pool, the Santa C is stuffed with knick-kna collected by the owne A few of the rooms at the back overlook a bu road, so try for the fro or middle of the house ◈ *Calçada do Pico 16B • Map N2 • 291 742 194 *

9 Residencial da Mariazinha

Funchal's oldest street slowly being restored the hope of attracting new business. This ho is one of the first resu a smart new residence with nine spacious roor and a suite with its ow jacuzzi. ◈ *Rua de Santa Maria 155 • Map P5 • 29 220 239 • www.residenc damariazinha.com • €€*

10 Pestana Carlton Madeira

This big tower block behind the Savoy wins no prizes for architectu but its garden and poo complex is equal to tho at any of the nearby luxury hotels. Opposite Reid's, it offers similar views for a lot less eur ◈ *Largo António Nobre • Map H6 • 291 239 500 • www.pestana.com • €€*

Note: Unless otherwise stated, all hotels accept credit cards, and have ensuite bathrooms and air conditioning

Price Categories

For a standard, double room per night (with breakfast if included), taxes and extra charges.

€ under €50
€€ €50–100
€€€ €100–150
€€€€ €150–200
€€€€€ over €200

...yal Orchid Hotel, Caniço de Baixo

10 Hotels in the East of the Island

1 Oasis Atlantic, Caniço de Baixo

...is big resort at the far ...d of the east district ...Caniço de Baixo has ...m, sauna, jacuzzi, ...door and outdoor pools ...d courtesy bus. ◈ ...Map J6 • 291 930 100 ...www.monumentallido ...asisatlantic.com • €€

2 Royal Orchid, Caniço de Baixo

...e of Caniço's newest ...xury hotels, the Royal ...rchid has almost ...erything you could ...int in a resort hotel, ...cluding rooms with ...ell-equipped kitchens ...d sea-view balconies. ...Travessa da Praia • Map ...• 291 934 600 • www. ...telroyalorchid.com • €€

3 Inn and Art, Caniço de Baixo

...e son of German artist ...egward Sprotte opened ...is "hotel gallery" in 1991 ...a place where artists ...uld stay, paint and ...splay their work. It has ...nce expanded beyond ...e original clifftop villa to ...clude several nearby ...ouses that can be rented ...r self-catering holidays, ...mplete with car. ...estaurant, heated pool, ...ga, fitness centre. ◈ ...ua Robert Baden Powell ...1/62 • Map J6 • 291 938 ...0 • www.innart.com • €€

4 Galomar, Caniço de Baixo

...n elevator links the main ...otel to an extensive lido ...t the base of Caniço's

towering cliffs. The lido is home to the Manta Diving School, so a fair proportion of guests choose the hotel in order to be able to dive in the rich marine reserve that surrounds the lido. ◈ Ponta da Oliveira • Map J6 • 291 930 930 • www.galo resorthotel.com • €€

5 Estalagem Serra Golf, Santo António da Serra

With its corner tower and stone balustrades, this eccentric 1920s house has been renovated into a relaxing country hotel perfectly located for the nearby Santo da Serra golf course. ◈ Casais Próximos • Map J4 • 291 550 500 • www.serragolf.com • €€

6 Estalagem do Santo, Santo António da Serra

This country inn with indoor pool, tennis court and pretty gardens makes a good base for exploring the east of the island. It's also close to the golf course at Santo da Serra. ◈ Casais Próximos • Map J4 • 291 550 550 • www. enotel.com • €€

7 Quinta do Furão, Santana

Rooms at this luxurious modern hotel enjoy breathtaking views along the rugged north coast of Madeira. Built on a head-land just on the edge of Santana, the hotel is surrounded by the vine-yards of the Madeira Wine Company. A bonus

for guests is the chance to tour the vineyards, and even help with the harvest if it's that time of year. Heated outdoor pool, sauna and gym. ◈ Achada do Gramacho • Map H2 • 291 570 100 • www. quintadofurao.com • €€€

8 Cabanas de São Jorge, São Jorge

The cabanas, or "cabins", are South African-style rondhovels ("round houses") set in peaceful gardens with dizzying clifftop views. This is an excellent place to break your journey and get to know the north coast. ◈ Beira da Quinta • Map H2 • 291 576 291 • www. cabanasvillage. com • €€

9 Solar de Boaventura, Boaventura

Tastefully converted from a classic Madeiran house dating back to 1776. The rooms are large. The restaurant serves local specialities. ◈ Serrão Boaventura • Map G2 • 291 860 888 • www.solar-boaventura.com • €€

10 Quinta do Lorde, Caniço de Baixo

Almost the very last habitation on the eastern peninsula of the island, the luxurious Quinta do Lorde has its own marina attracting weekend sailors from Funchal and voyagers from both sides of the Atlantic. ◈ Sítio da Piedade • Map J6 • 291 960 200 • €€€€€

Left **Jardim Atlântico** Right **Quinta do Alto de São João**

Hotels in the West of the Island

1 Quinta do Estreito, Câmara de Lobos

This was once the main wine estate in the area. The old house is now the setting for the Bacchus gourmet restaurant and the Vintage bar and library; the old wine lodge now houses the Adega da Quinta restaurant serving Madeiran country food. Modern guest quarters are set in landscaped gardens with olive grove and organic vegetable plot. ✪ *Rua José Joaquim da Costa • Map F6 • 291 910 530 •www.charming hotelsmadeira.com • €€€€*

2 Estalagem da Ponta do Sol, Ponta do Sol

Swap bright city lights for views of the setting sun from this stylish clifftop hotel. Distinctive bridges and towers link modern guest quarters with the more traditional bar and library area and the glass-walled rest-aurant. Swimming pool, gym and courtesy bus. ✪ *Quinta da Rochinha • Map D5 • 291 970 200 • www. pontadosol.com • €€*

3 Baía do Sol, Ponta do Sol

In 2002, the Ponta do Sol seafront was redeveloped to create this hotel, which cleverly retains all the old façades that have graced the palm-lined esplanade since the 19th century. ✪ *Rua Dr João Augusto Teixeira • Map D5 • 291 970 140 • www.enotel.com • €€*

4 Quinta do Alto de São João, Ponta do Sol

Open your window and hear nothing but the bees at work in the manor gardens. With a set daily menu and attentive staff, you will feel like a guest in the home of an absent aristocrat. ✪ *Lomba de São João • Map D5 • 291 974 188 • www.qasj.cjb.net • €€*

5 Jardim Atlântico, Prazeres

The remoteness of this hotel is part of its charm. Guests are encouraged to explore the surrounding coast and countryside. Rooms, complete with kitchens, are huge. There is a mini-market on site. ✪ *Lomba da Rocha • Map B3 • 291 820 220 • www. jardimatlantico.com • €€€*

6 Pousada dos Vinháticos, Serra de Água

This small country inn sits on a saddle of rock between two of the island's most majestic groups of mountains. There is no better way to end the day on Madeira than with drinks on the hotel terrace as the setting sun lights up the west-facing peaks. ✪ *Map E4 • 291 952 344 • www.dorisol.pt • €€*

7 Residencial Encumeada, Serra de Água

A little higher up the valley than the Pousada dos Vinháticos, this modern hotel boasts fine views. Surrounded by natural laurel forest, it is close to some of the best *levada* and mountain paths that the island has to offer. ✪ *Feiteiras • Map E4 • 291 951 282 • www.residencial encumeada.com • €*

8 Estalagem Eira do Serrado, Eira do Serrado

The northern façade of this small mountain hotel consists of nothing but glass, so that diners in the restaurant and overnight guests in the simply furnished rooms can drink their fill of the spectacular views of the Curral das Freiras and its encircling cliffs *(see p30)*. ✪ *Map G4 • 291 710 060 • www. eiradoserrado.com • €€*

9 Residencial Calhau, Porto Moniz

There are lots of newer, better equipped hotels in Porto Moniz, but none whose seaward walls are built out onto the rocky foreshore, so that you can fall asleep to the soothing sound of the waves. ✪ *Sítio das Poças • Map B1 • 291 853 104 •*

10 Residencial O Farol, Ponta do Pargo

If you make it this far west, you can unwind at this simple hotel between the village and the cliffs ✪ *Salão de Baixo • Map A1 • 291 880 010 • €*

Note: Unless otherwise stated, all hotels accept credit cards, and have ensuite bathrooms and air conditioning

Price Categories
For a standard,
double room per
night (with breakfast
if included), taxes
and extra charges.

€ under €50
€€ €50–100
€€€ €100–150
€€€€ €150–200
€€€€€ over €200

...enue Park self-catering apartments

10 Self-catering and Budget Hotels

1 Suite Hotel Eden Mar, Funchal

...e Eden Mar offers ...od-value self-catering ...well-furnished rooms ...th small kitchens. It ...so provides access to ...e of Madeira's best ...sort complexes, the ...rto Mare *(see p112)*. *Rua do Gorgulho 2 Map G6 • 291 709 700 www.edenmar.com • €€€*

2 Monumental Lido, Funchal

...e well-priced rooms at ...s pleasant hotel in the ...tel Zone have separate ...tchens and living areas; ...edrooms face onto a ...iet inner atrium. Shops ...d the Lido are nearby. *Estrada Monumental 284 Map G6 • 291 724 000 www.monumentallido.com €€€*

3 Avenue Park, Funchal

...e spacious, light and ...ell-furnished apartment ...oms at this self-catering ...stablishment close to ...e centre of downtown ...nchal are a real bargain. ...e underground garage ...a bonus. *Avda do ...fante 26D • Map Q1 291 205 630 • www. ...adeiraapartments.com/ ...enuepark • €€*

4 Quinta Vale do Til, Campanário

...or rural self-catering, ...e Quinta Vale do Til has ...e advantage of being ...cated on its own private ...state. It sleeps eight, in ...ur double bedrooms.

Boa Morte, São João • Map E5 • 291 910 530 • www.charminghotels madeira.com • €€

5 Rental Agencies

Two websites carry links to self-catering accommodation for rent by the week: Madeira Online and Madeira Island. The Summer Bureau has details of apartments, studios and bungalows, largely in Caniço de Baixo. *www.madeiraonline. com • www.madeira- island.com • Summer Bureau: Rua D Francesco Sanatana, Caniço de Baixo. Map J6. 291 934 519*

6 Bed-and-breakfast

English-style bed-and-breakfast has been taken to Madeira by Trevor and June Franks. Trejuno, their guesthouse, is midway between Funchal and Monte. Walking tips, free airport pickup, and inside information. *Estrada do Livramento 94 • Map H5 • 291 783 268 • www. tjwalking-madeira.com • €€*

7 Camping

Officially, camping is illegal on Madeira, except at two designated sites. One is at Porto Moniz, where new facilities are under construction. The other is on Porto Santo, alongside the Torre Praia Hotel – advance booking is recommended in July and August. *Porto Moniz tourist office: 291 850 193 • Porto Santo campsite: 291 982 160 • €*

8 Budget Accommodation in Funchal

The following are clean, quiet and cheap *pensões, residenciais* and hotels in the heart of town. *Astória: Rua de João Gago 10. Map P3. 291 223 820. € • do Centro: Rua do Carmo 20. Map P4. 291 200 510. € • Monaco: Rua das Hortas 14A. Map N4. 291 222 667. € • Sirius: Rua das Hortas 29. Map N4. 291 226 117. € • Residencial Zarco: Rua da Alfândega 113. Map P3. 291 223 716. €*

9 Budget Accommodation Outside of Funchal

The Hortensia Gardens *(see p79)* offers cheap accommodation within its peaceful gardens. Boa Vista Orchids *(see p56)* has a thatched cottage for three. At O Escon-didinho das Canas in Santana, you can sleep in a traditional A-shaped cottage. *Hortensia Gardens: www.madeira island.com/hotels/self_cater ing_apartments/hortensia. € • Boa Vista Orchids: Quinta da Boa Vista, Rua Lombo da Boa Vista, Funchal. Map H5. 291 220 468. €€ • O Escon-didinho das Canas: Pico António Fernandes, Santana. Map H2. 291 572 319. €*

10 Rural Tourism

Madeira Rural is an online booking agent for 20 or so properties around the island, from converted farm buildings to cottages. *www.madeira-rural.com*

General Index

Phrase Book

In an Emergency

Help!	Socorro!	soo-**koh**-roo
Stop!	Páre!	pahr'
Call a doctor!	Chame um médico!	**shahm'** ooñ **meh**-dee-koo
Call an ambulance!	Chame uma ambulância!	**shahm'** oo-muh añ-boo-**lañ**-see-uh
Call the police!	Chame a polícia!	**shahm'** uh poo-**lee**-see-uh
Call the fire brigade!	Chame os bombeiros!	**shahm'** oosh bom-**bay**-roosh
Where is the nearest telephone?	Há um telefone aqui perto?	**ah** ooñ te-le-**fon'** uh-**kee pehr**-too
Where is the nearest hospital?	Onde é o hospital mais próximo?	ond' **eh** oo **ohsh**-pee-**tahl' mysh pro**-see-moo

Communication Essentials

Yes	Sim	seeñ
No	Não	nowñ
Please	Por favor/ Faz favor	poor fuh-**vor**/ fash fuh-**vor**
Thank you	Obrigado/da	o-bree-**gah**-doo/duh
Excuse me	Desculpe	dish-**koolp'**
Hello	Olá	oh-**lah**
Goodbye	Adeus	a-**deh**-oosh
Good morning	Bom-dia	boñ **dee**-uh
Good afternoon	Boa-tarde	boh-uh tard'
Good night	Boa-noite	boh-uh noyt'
Yesterday	Ontem	oñ-**tayñ**
Today	Hoje	ohj'
Tomorrow	Amanhã	ah-man **yañ**
Here	Aqui	uh-**kee**
There	Ali	uh-**lee**
What?	O quê?	oo keh
Which?	Qual?	kwahl'
When?	Quando?	**kwañ**-doo
Why?	Porquê?	**poor**-keh
Where?	Onde?	oñd'

Useful Phrases

How are you?	Como está?	**koh**-moo shtah
Very well, thank you.	Bem, obrigado/da.	bayñ o-bree-**gah**-doo/duh
Pleased to meet you.	Encantado/da.	eñ-kañ-**tah**-doo/ duh
See you soon.	Até logo.	uh-**teh loh**-goo
That's fine.	Está bem.	shtah bayñ
Where is/are...?	Onde está/ estão...?	ond' shtah/ shtowñ
How far is it to...?	A que distância fica...?	uh kee dish-**tañ**-see-uh **fee**-kuh
Which way to...?	Como se vai para...?	**koh**-moo seh **vy** puh-ruh
Do you speak English?	Fala Inglês?	**fah**-luh eeñ-**glehsh**
I don't understand.	Não compreendo.	nowñ kom-pree-**en**-doo
I'm sorry.	Desculpe.	dish-**koolp'**
Could you speak more slowly please?	Pode falar mais devagar por favor?	**pohd'** fuh-**lar** mysh d'-va-**gar** poor fah-**vor**

Sightseeing

cathedral	sé	seh
church	igreja	ee-**gray**-juh
garden	jardim	jar-**deeñ**
library	biblioteca	bee-blee-oo-**teh**-kuh
museum	museu	moo-**zeh**-oo
tourist information	posto de turismo	**posh**-too d' too-**reesh**-mi
closed for holidays	fechado para férias	fe-**sha**-doo puh-ruh **feh**-ree-ash
bus station	estação de autocarros	shta-sowñ d' too-**kah**-roos
railway station	estação de comboios	shta-**sowñ** d' koñ-**boy**-oos
azulejo	uh-zoo-**lay**-joo	painted cerar tile
Manuelino	ma-noo-el-**ee**-noo	Manueline (la Gothic archi-tectural style

Useful Words

big	grande	grand'
small	pequeno	pe-**keh**-noo
hot	quente	kent'
cold	frio	**free**-oo
good	bom	boñ
bad	mau	**mah**-oo
enough	bastante	bash-**tant'**
well	bem	bayñ
open	aberto	a-**behr**-too
closed	fechado	fe-**shah**-doo
left	esquerda	**shkehr**-duh
right	direita	dee-**ray**-tuh
straight on	em frente	ayñ **frent'**
near	perto	**pehr**-too
far	longe	loñj'
up	suba	**soo**-bah
down	desça	**deh**-shuh
early	cedo	**seh**-doo
late	tarde	tard'
entrance	entrada	en-**trah**-duh
exit	saída	sa-**ee**-duh
toilets	casa de banho	**kah**-zuh d' **ban**-yoo
more	mais	mysh
less	menos	**meh**-noosh

Shopping

How much does this cost?	Quanto custa isto?	**kwan**-too **koosh**-tuh **eesh**-too
I would like... I'm just looking.	Queria... Estou só a ver obrigado/a.	**kree**-uh **shtoh soh** uh **vehr** o-bree-**gah**-doo/uh
Do you take credit cards?	Aceita cartões de crédito?	uh-**say**-tuh **toinsh** de **kreh**-dee-too
What time do you open?	A que horas abre?	uh **kee oh**-r **ah**-bre?
What time do you close?	A que horas fecha?	uh **kee oh**-r **fay**-shuh?
this one	este	ehst'
that one	esse	ehss'
expensive	caro	**kah**-roo

	barato	buh-**rah**-too
(clothes/ es)	número	noom'-roo
	branco	**brañ**-koo
	preto	**preh**-too
	roxo	**roh**-shoo
w	amarelo	uh-muh-**reh**-loo
n	verde	vehrd'
	azul	uh-**zool**'

es of Shop

ue shop	loja de antiguidades	**loh**-juh de an-tee-gwee-**dahd**'sh
ry	padaria	pah-duh-**ree**-uh
	banco	**bañ**-koo
shop	livraria	lee-vruh-**ree**-uh
her	talho	**tah**-lyoo
shop	pastelaria	pash-te-luh-**ree**-uh
nist	farmácia	far-**mah**-see-uh
nonger	peixaria	pay-shuh-**ree**-uh
dresser	cabeleireiro	kab'-lay-**ray**-roo
et	mercado	mehr-**kah**-doo
sagent	kiosque	kee-**yohsk**'
office	correios	koo-**ray**-oosh
shop	sapataria	suh-puh-tuh-**ree**-uh
rmarket	supermercado	**soo**-pehr-mer-**kah**-doo
cconist	tabacaria	tuh-buh-kuh-**ree**-uh
agency	agência de viagens	uh-jeñ-**see**-uh de vee-**ah**-jayñsh

ying in a Hotel

ou have acant room?	Tem um quarto livre?	tayñ ooñ **kwar**-too **leev**r'
n with ath	um quarto com casa de banho	ooñ **kwar**-too koñ **kah**-zuh d' ban-**yoo**
ver	duche	doosh
e room	quarto individual	**kwar**-too een-dee-vee-doo-**ahl**'
ble room	quarto de casal	**kwar**-too d' kuh-**zhal**'
room	quarto com duas camas	**kwar**-too koñ doo-ash **kah**-mash
er	porteiro chave	poor-**tay**-roo shahv'
ve a ervation.	Tenho um quarto reservado.	**tayn**-yoo ooñ **kwar**-too re-ser-**vah**-doo

ing Out

e you a table ...?	Tem uma mesa para ... ?	tayñ oo-muh **meh**-zuh puh-ruh
a etarian.	Sou vegetariano/a.	Soh ve-je-tuh-ree-**ah**-noo/uh
er!	Por favor!/ Faz favor!	poor fuh-**vor**/ fash fuh-**vor**
ke to erve a table.	Quero reservar una mesa.	**keh**-roo re-zehr-**var** oo-muh **meh**-zuh

The bill, please.	A conta por favor/faz favor.	uh **kohn**-tuh poor fuh-**vor**/ fash fuh-**vor**
the menu	a lista	uh **leesh**-tuh
fixed-price menu	a ementa turística	uh ee-**mehn**-tuh too-**reesh**-tee-kuh
wine list	a lista de vinhos	uh **leesh**-tuh de **veen**-yoosh
glass	um copo	ooñ **koh**-poo
bottle	uma garrafa	oo-muh guh-**rah**-fuh
half bottle	meia-garrafa	**may**-uh guh-**rah**-fuh
knife	uma faca	oo-mah **fah**-kuh
fork	um garfo	ooñ **gar**-foo
spoon	uma colher	oo-muh kool-**yair**
plate	um prato	ooñ **prah**-too
breakfast	pequeno-almoço	pe-**keh**-noo-ahl-**moh**-soo
lunch	almoço	ahl-**moh**-soo
dinner	jantar	jan-**tar**
cover	couvert	koo-**vehr**
starter	entrada	en-**trah**-duh
main course	prato principal	**prah**-too prin-see-**pahl**'
dish of the day	prato do dia	**prah**-too doo **dee**-uh
set dish	combinado	koñ-bee-**nah**-doo
half portion	meia-dose	may-uh **doh**-se
dessert	sobremesa	soh-bre-**meh**-zuh
rare	mal passado	**mahl**' puh-**sah**-doo
medium	médio	**meh**-dee-oo
well done	bem passado	**bayñ** puh-**sah**-doo

Menu Decoder

abacate	uh-buh-**kaht**'	avocado
açorda	uh-**sor**-duh	bread- and garlic-based soup
açúcar	uh-**soo**-kuhr	sugar
água mineral	**ah**-gwuh mee-ne-**rahl**'	mineral water
alho	**ahl**-yoo	garlic
alperce	ahl'-**pehrce**	apricot
amêijoas	uh-**may**-joo-ush	clams
ananás	uh-nuh-**nahsh**	pineapple
anona	ah-**noh**-nah	custard apple
arroz	uh-**rohsh**	rice
assado	uh-**sah**-doo	baked
atum	uh-**tooñ**	tuna
aves	**ah**-vesh	poultry
azeite	uh-**zayt**'	olive oil
azeitonas	uh-zay-**toh**-nash	olives
bacalhau	buh-kuh-**lyow**	dried, salted cod
banana	buh-**nah**-nuh	banana
batatas	buh-**tah**-tash	potatoes
batatas fritas	buh-**tah**-tash **free**-tash	french fries
batido	buh-**tee**-doo	milk-shake
bica	**bee**-kuh	espresso
bife	beef	beef
bolacha	boo-**lah**-shuh	biscuit
bolo	**boh**-loo	cake
bolo de caco	**boh**-loo d' **kah**-koh	Madeiran bread

caça	**kah**-ssuh	game
café	kuh-**feh**	coffee
camarões	kuh-muh-**roysh**	large prawns
carangueijo	kuh-rañ **gay**-yoo	crab
carne	**karn'**	meat
castanhas	cash-**tahn**-yush	chestnuts
cebola	se-**boh**-luh	onion
cerejas	sehr-**ray**-jahs	cherries
cerveja	sehr-**vay**-juh	beer
chá	**shah**	tea
cherne	**shern'**	stone bass
chinesa	shee-**neh**-zuh	white coffee
chocolate	shoh-koh-**laht'**	chocolate
chocos	**shoh**-koosh	cuttlefish
chouriço	shoh-**ree**-soo	red, spicy sausage
churrasco	shoo-**rash**-coo	on the spit
coelho	koo-**el**-yoo	rabbit
cogumelos	koo-goo-**meh**-loosh	mushrooms
cordeiro	kur-**deh**-roo	lamb
cozido	koo-**zee**-doo	boiled
dourada	doh-**rah**-dah	sea bream
espada	(e)sh-**pah**-dah	scabbard fish
espetada	(e)sh-puh-**tah**-dah	Madeiran beef kebab
espadarte	(e)sh-pah-**dahr**-tuh	swordfish
fiambre	fee-**ambri**	ham
frango	**fran**-goo	chicken
frito	**free**-too	fried
fruta	**froo**-tuh	fruit
gambas	**gam**-bash	prawns
gelado	je-**lah**-doo	ice cream
gelo	**jeh**-loo	ice
goiaba	goy-**ah**-bah	guava
grelhado	grel-**yah**-doo	grilled
kiwi	**kee**-wee	kiwi fruit
lagosta	luh-**gohsh**-tuh	lobster
lapas	**lah**-push	limpets
laranja	luh **rañ**-juh	orange
leite	**layt'**	milk
limão	lee-**mowñ**	lemon
limonada	lee-moo-**nah**-duh	lemonade
linguado	leeñ-**gwah**-doo	sole
lulas	**loo**-lash	squid
maçã	muh-**sañ**	apple
manga	**mahn**-gah	mango
manteiga	mañ-**tay**-guh	butter
maracujá	muhr-ah-koo-**jah**	passion fruit
mariscos	muh-**reesh**-koosh	seafood
milho frito	**meel**-yoo **free**-too	deep-fried cubes of maize meal
morangos	moh-**rahn**-gosh	strawberries
ostras	**osh**-trash	oysters
ovos	**oh**-voosh	eggs
pão	**powñ**	bread
pargo	**pahr**-goo	red bream
pastel	pash-**tehl'**	cake
peixe	**paysh'**	fish
pêssego	**pess**-eh-goo	peach
pêssego	**pess**-eh-goo	nectarine
careca	kah-**ray**-kuh	
pimenta	pee-**men**-tuh	pepper
polvo	**pohl'**-voo	octopus
porco	**por**-coo	pork
prego	**pray**-goh	steak sandwich
queijo	**kay**-joo	cheese
sal	**sahl'**	salt
salada	suh-**lah**-duh	salad
salsichas	sahl-**see**-shash	sausages
sandes	**san**-desh	sandwich
sopa	**soh**-puh	soup
sumo	**soo**-moo	juice

tamboril	tam-boo-**ril'**	monkfish
tarte	**tart'**	pie/cake
tamarilho	tahm-ah-**reel**-yoo	tomarillo
tomate	too-**maht'**	tomato
torrada	too-**rah**-duh	toast
tosta	**tohsh**-tuh	toasted sandwich
vinagre	vee-**nah**-gre	vinegar
vinho branco	**veen**-yoo **brañ**-koo	white wine
vinho tinto	**veen**-yoo **teen**-too	red wine
vitela	vee-**teh**-luh	veal

Numbers

0	zero	**zeh**-roo
1	um	**ooñ**
2	dois	**doysh**
3	três	**tresh**
4	quatro	**kwa**-troo
5	cinco	**seeñ**-koo
6	seis	**saysh**
7	sete	**set'**
8	oito	**oy**-too
9	nove	**nov'**
10	dez	de-**esh**
11	onze	**oñz'**
12	doze	**doz'**
13	treze	**trez'**
14	catorze	ka-**torz'**
15	quinze	**keeñz'**
16	dezasseis	de-zuh-**say**
17	dezassete	de-zuh-**se**
18	dezoito	de-**zoy**-too
19	dezanove	de-zuh-**no**
20	vinte	**veent'**
21	vinte e um	**veen-tee-**
30	trinta	**treeñ**-tuh
40	quarenta	kwa-**ren**-tuh
50	cinquenta	seen-**kwen**
60	sessenta	se-**sen**-tuh
70	setenta	se-**ten**-tuh
80	oitenta	oy-**ten**-tuh
90	noventa	noo-**ven**-tu
100	cem	**sayñ**
101	cento e um	**sen**-too-ee
102	cento e dois	**sen**-too-ee doysh
200	duzentos	doo-**zen**-tc
300	trezentos	tre-**zen**-toc
400	quatrocentos	**kwa**-troo-s toosh
500	quinhentos	kee-**nyen-t**
600	seiscentos	saysh-**sen-**
700	setecentos	set'-**sen**-tor
800	oitocentos	oy-too-**sen** toosh
900	novecentos	nov'-**sen**-tc
1,000	mil	**meel'**

Time

one minute	um minuto	ooñ mee-**n** too
one hour	uma hora	oo-muh **oh**
half an hour	meia-hora	**may**-uh oh
Monday	segunda-feira	se-**goon**-de **fay**-ruh
Tuesday	terça-feira	ter-sa-**fay**-r
Wednesday	quarta-feira	kwar-ta-**fay**
Thursday	quinta-feira	keen-ta-**fay**
Friday	sexta-feira	say-shta-**fa** ruh
Saturday	sábado	**sah**-ba-too
Sunday	domingo	doo-**meeñ**-g

cknowledgements

Author

topher Catling has written more than
avel guides, including best-selling DK
itness guides to Florence and Venice.
lso contributed to the Portugal, Italy
Great Britain guides in the same series.
n not writing books, he works as an
eologist and heritage consultant. He
Fellow of the Society of Antiquaries
he Royal Society of Arts, and a member
e British Guild of Travel Writers. He
s Madeira, and never grows tired of
ng it to walk, and to enjoy the food
warm hospitality of the islanders.

ial thanks for their invaluable assistance
abel Góis at the Madeira Tourist Board in
hal and Elsa Cortez at the Portuguese
nal Tourist Office in London.

duced by DP Services, a division of
CAN PETERSEN PUBLISHING LTD,
eylon Road, London W14 0PY

ect Editor Chris Barstow
igner Ian Midson
ure Researcher Lily Sellar
ings Researcher Tomas Tranæus
exer Hilary Bird
ofreader Yoko Kawaguchi
n Photographer Antony Souter
itional Photography Linda Whitwam
strator Chapel Design & Marketing
s John Plumer, JP Map Graphics

ography Credits
eira base map derived from Madeira
ist Board, www.madeiratourism.org

DORLING KINDERSLEY
lisher Douglas Amrine
ior Art Editor Tessa Bindloss
ior Cartographic Editor Casper Morris
ior DTP Designer Jason Little
duction Linda Dare
ure Librarian Romaine Werblow

Revisions Coordinator Mani Ramaswamy
Assistant Revisions Coordinator
Mary Ormandy
Design and Editorial Assistance Sangita
Patel, Marianne Petrou, Tomas Tranæus.

Picture Credits
Placement Key: t-top; tc-top centre; tl-top
left; tr-top right; cla-centre left above; ca-
centre above; cra-centre right above; cl-
centre left; c-centre; cr-centre right; clb-
centre left below; cb-centre below; crb-
centre right below; bl-below left; bc-below
centre; br-below right; b-bottom.

Every effort has been made to trace the
copyright holders and we apologise in
advance for any unintentional omissions.
We would be pleased to insert the
appropriate acknowledgements in any
subsequent edition of this publication.

The publishers would like to thank the
following individuals, companies and
picture libraries for permission to
reproduce their photographs:

ALAMY: Robert Harding Picture Library
32–33c; Ernst Wrba 29b; MADEIRA
TOURISM: 30b, 54tl, 54tr, 55bl, 55cr;
MARTIN SIEPMANN: 23b, 33cra; MARY
EVANS PICTURE LIBRARY: 37tr, 37bl;
MICHELLE CHAPLOW: 61tr, 61br; MUSEU
DE ARTE SACRA DO FUNCHAL: 10b;
NATIONAL MARITIME MUSEUM,
LONDON: 36c; POWERSTOCK: 54cl;
PRISMA: 92–93; THE SAVOY RESORT,
Funchal, Madeira Island: All rights
reserved. 112tr; TOMAS TRANÆUS: 71;
TOPFOTO: 37cr, 37br.

For jacket credits see Contents page.

All other images are © Dorling Kindersley.
For further information see
www.dkimages.com

Selected Index of Places